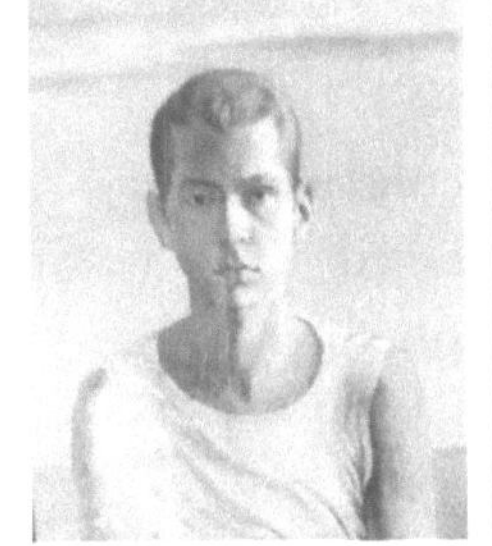
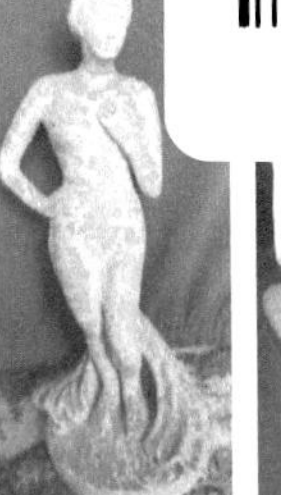

My Name Is Bill, Not Buddy

STEPHANIE FISHER

NEWMAN SPRINGS PUBLISHING
320 Broad Street
Red Bank, NJ 07701

First originally published by Newman Springs Publishing 2024

ISBN 979-8-89061-607-4 (Paperback)
ISBN 979-8-89061-608-1 (Digital)

Printed in the United States of America

This book is dedicated to my family members, both living and those that are no longer with us. The strength that I received from them all is part of the reason that this book came to be. I am truly blessed to have loving and supportive family members, and I do realize that is not always the case for everyone.

To my girls, you continue to be the reason that I will try to be the best version of myself and to set the best example of love, devotion, and acceptance that I can achieve. I will always be yearning to improve for the better.

Stephanie

ACKNOWLEDGMENT

Bill, I am so grateful that you were your true self, with no apologies, and lived your life to the fullest. You were a wonderful example of how we should all be. The gratitude that I found in life and myself from this experience, I will treasure and share with anyone that is willing to listen and continue to move forward.

I will continue to be an ally to those in the LGBTQ+ community and always try to educate myself and others to help provide the best possible support that I can, in your name and for all others who have been made to feel less deserving of all the things that life has to offer.

LAND ACKNOWLEDGMENTS

I am grateful to live and work on the lands of indigenous people, specifically Cayuse, Wanapum, Nez Perce, Confederated Tribes of the Yakama Nation, Confederated Tribes of Umatilla Indian Reservation, and Walla Walla tribes. From my family history, I must include the Choctaw and Chickasaw tribes as well. As guests of this land in both the past, present, and in the future, we recognize their presence since time long-established and dedicate ourselves to steward this land and to continue education about indigenous communities.

Dear William "Buddy" Chauncey Kolb,

Okay, how do I start this off…I am your great-niece, and we never got the chance to meet face-to-face. Well, that is not 100 percent the truth. I am writing letters to express my love and adoration for your life that I was not able to be a part of, and I will try to add a small copy of a picture that means something to me about you. You were taken from us too soon, and this is a way I can feel connected to you. With this letter, I have two favorites that have helped me get started. I did find a picture that has you and me in it, sort of. The family picture with the dark-haired woman on the right is my mother, Patsy, and she just happened to be pregnant with me. So I guess we were in a picture together. You are on the left and looking stoic. This was the only time that we would be together, directly or indirectly. It puts a smile on my face to know that I have this one moment captured in time that we were together, and I can revisit whenever I want.

There are lots of favorites, so I will try to stick with my top picks. This is one of my all-time favorite pictures of you. You look so handsome, thoughtful, and kind. It sounds funny to say that by just looking at the picture. I know that it is impossible to read behind what lies in someone else's eyes. However, from looking at all the photo albums, articles, and works of art, I feel that can say and see these qualities. I have lots of things that I wish I had been able to speak about with you.

I understand that you will never see these letters, but I am hoping that writing to you will help ease my pain and help me find answers to questions that were either never asked or never investigated further. Someone took you from us in a way that was truly unforgivable. I thought that by creating letters, it would help me feel closer to you since I wasn't given that opportunity while you were alive. I am only able to look through our family history, remember old stories told by family members, and then I try my best to put the puzzle pieces of your life together. Putting a puzzle together without having the big picture is never easy, but it still can be just as rewarding. As I went through everything, I noticed that there was so much that we didn't know about you or so much that wasn't talked about. That could have been by your choice or from lack of understanding from others; either way, I am grateful that I have taken this underway and that I am learning as much as I can about you and your life. The more I find out about you, the more intrigued I am. This anonymous quote sums up my feelings about the gratitude that I feel in taking on this challenge to find out about you, "It is not happiness that brings us gratitude. It's gratitude that brings us happiness."

One of the first things that jumped out at me was the issue with your name and what you wanted to be called. When you reached adulthood, you had announced that you would want to go by the name Bill, and not the name that was gifted to you, Buddy. Your birth name, William Chauncey, was given to you by your mother: Chauncey was after your own father, and William for his maternal grandfather, William Alfred Wagner. They tried to fulfill your wishes; however, it would not come to pass. You kindly but begrudgingly gave in and obliged your family and put your needs aside, telling your mother that it was okay, you would just be "Buddy." I have a feeling that you had to do that a lot in your life, didn't you? I know that the name Buddy happened because of your older brother, Jack, my grandfather. Jack was only two years old when they brought you home. When Jack went to the hospital, he went right up to you and placed a prize marble in your tiny little fist. He called you my little buddy, and the name stuck. I think I would have enjoyed seeing the two of you together, and I would have seen a much different side of my grandfather. You were such a stark opposite of your brother, my stern and serious grandfather Jack.

One giant aspect of your life that I am inspired by is that you knew wholeheartedly who you were and where you were going. You were asked at age five what you wanted to grow up and become, and you answered that you would be a bus driver in New York City. None of the family at the time knew where on earth you had heard of New York City; however, it was the city that you loved, lived, worked, and died in. Some people just know who and what they are going to be, and that was you! You weren't a bus driver, but you wanted to live in New York City, and so you did! Very few of our family members have visited the city that you loved so much.

Another thing that surprised me while looking into your past, I was not aware of the sire amount of traveling and relocating that our family has been involved in. From living in different parts of Texas and Oklahoma to traveling to Richmond, Virginia, and then later to New York City and Washington State. Quite honestly, I can't believe that I live in Washington State; it is only based on Jack's decision to take a job out here. The last time that you were photographed in Washington State was in the mid-1970s. Unfortunately, I started learning about you when I was in high school and college, when I would visit with family and speak briefly, but the conversation never got too far. From what they told me, you truly had an exceptional eye to make anything beautiful! I would have loved to talk with you about any of your works of art, experiences, and what life was like in New York.

I grew up looking at all your works of art around my great grandmother, your mother, Lena, Mimi's and Jack's houses. You left so much beauty behind with the multitude of work that you created. You wrote poetry at a very young age; you were an artist, portrait painter, sculptor, created special effects, designed, and rendered presentation sketches, merchandising props, and decorative displays for all major department stores and chain stores, created decor for store windows for both interior and exterior. Some of your portraits are displayed on the walls of many beautiful homes in Virginia; New York; Westport, Connecticut; Illinois; New Mexico; Tennessee; Missouri; Washington, DC; Texas; London, England; and the British West Indies. I would love to see them or at least find out if they are still there. There are probably more, but I will get to that later.

From the gentle way you allowed everyone to call you by the same name, I know that you truly were one of a kind and sacrificed parts of yourself to be where you wanted to be. I believe that dreams, people, and other life-inspiring things do come true. Without sacrifice and discipline, we tend to stay in the same place. It was the only place where you could be your authentic self. I know that this will sound silly, but I wanted to create a safe space here in our correspondence. I would like to think that you could answer me and tell me how you feel. I hope that every place you went to, you found people that surrounded you with love, support, and understanding.

Instead of being cruel and distant through the many ups and downs of your life, you were instead generous, funny, and the kind of person people wanted to be around, and you channeled it into your art and lived the best life that you could. I wanted to do some acts of kindness for others in your name's sake. I feel as if that is one way that I can honor your memory and keep a part of you with me. In your name, I am going to make conscious choices to educate myself and find ways to better support those that are not represented or who are discriminated in our communities. I will research lingo for inclusivity, history or timeline information, and ways that I can be an active ally. I feel like this would not only be a better way to heal from your loss but an opportunity to help others that are going through similar experiences. This can be the way to heal by loving and supporting others. For you, for me, and anyone else that these letters might come across.

As for me, I am a teacher, and it can be difficult to navigate through some of these issues, especially being supportive to those who tend to be marginalized in my profession. Teachers are being told on all fronts how to do their job. I find it funny—not ha-ha funny but funny nonetheless—that people from all walks of life and in all kinds of career paths feel that it is their job to inform an educator what they should be doing in the classroom. I would never go up to someone else while they are working, or during the time that they are preparing for their work, to stop them and tell them how to do something that I know they already know how to get the job done. I would do what I am about to do myself: educate, research, and ask questions if I can't find what I am looking for. This indifference or inability to stop oneself from opening one's mouth and just spewing their opinion to a knowledgeable person seems so infringing, it becomes too much to process. We must do better for everyone's sakes.

So I will start with this for you. Very simply, you wanted your loved ones to call you by your name, and during your life, that request was denied. I know that this was one of many pieces of your life that you had to give in for the sake of others' comfort. Unfortunately, we all have trade-offs in this life. Whether it be time, money, or anything else from life, it happens. In these letters that I am sending you, you will not have to be someone else. You can truly be yourself.

Maybe you found that in New York City all those years ago. I hope so. There will not be any times or date on any of these. I just want to send them to you as they come from my heart. I wish that I had been able to meet you; however, you were taken from us in the cruelest way, and I was not given the chance. To make things right from this injustice we have suffered, I will also push myself and do acts of kindness and support in your name to help others that have had to hide who they are for fear of not being accepted or loved because they walk in their truth. No one should have to hide who they are or be less for someone's else comfort. I will do for you what others couldn't, and from here on out, I will refer to you by the name that you wanted to be called, Bill. Knowing this, I will continue to look for answers about what happened to you. Oh, sweet Bill, you are loved and missed. I will write to you again soon.

With all my love,
Stephanie (your great-niece)

PS—For my first act of kindness and support, I am following a group called LGBT Life Center on social media, and they are providing support to the LGBTQ+ community by affirming support groups to help reduce isolation and stigma. They have events, testing and health information, life blogs, how to get involved, and other services. Their overall goal is to help individuals learn healthy relationship skills, get further support on coming out, explore sexual orientation and gender identity, and connect with others (LGBT Life Center 2023).

PPS—I have found some other works of art that belong to you that I would like to end each letter with. I enjoyed looking through all the beautiful pieces of art that our family has saved over the years. Here is a poem that I liked too!

My Bird Poem

If I were a bird with wings so bright,
I'd fly and fly, fly all night.
If I were a bird with a song so sweet,
I'd play where the flowers greet.
And if I were the mockingbird,
with songs so gay,
Even if he is a dingy gray,
If I were a bird as jolly as he,
I'd play away up in a tree.
The blue-jay is an awful thing,
He doesn't even try to sing.
He squawks and squawks and squawks all day,
I believe that is all that he can say.
The birdies are the sweetest things,
For they all like to sing.
They wouldn't hurt you for a piece of bread,
And then some boys shoot them dead.
I like the mocker, best of all,
He always sings in the fall.

The chee-chee has a dear little
song,
But it doesn't last so very long.

—Wm. C. Kolb

CHAPTER 1

Mimi (Lena)

Dearest Bill,

Your mother, my great-grandmother, Lena, or I should say, Mimi, was something else. I am looking at this picture that I am sending with the letter, and she was such a force of nature. She knew what she wanted and went all out for it. No excuses, no exceptions, just her. That is who you got it from; since I know very little about Chauncey, I am left with this belief. She could be funny and kind on one hand and harsh and commanding the very next. We all know someone like her in our lives; some of us are extra lucky if we happen to be related to them. She was very connected to animals, especially dogs. Witnessing her connection with dogs as a young child is one of the reasons I care for dogs so much. She did like cats as well, but Mimi had a true love for dogs that I remember so fondly, and more importantly, the dogs knew that and loved her too. I remember Jack's hunting dogs, which he did have a few, would love to go over to Mimi's house and receive all the love and treats that she could give them. They were so excited that they would almost knock her over.

I remember a few times when I was visiting, I would have to make sure that she was sitting down in her favorite chair, and then I would let Jack know that all was clear, and he would let them in. They would come bounding down her backdoor hallway into her living room, and I would make sure that all art or breakables were put in high-enough places so their tails wouldn't smash them into a million pieces. It was so cute to see how happy she would get when they came up to her and licked her face or tried to sit in her lap. They just knew that she loved them, too, and Jack was not always the most affectionate, but he did love them, too, in his own way.

The dogs that I remember the most were Red, Frisky, and Princess. Princess was Jack's favorite and pride-and-joy dog. She was a regal hunting dog and did everything to perfection; however, she passed away, and I remember how upsetting that was to him. It was an emotion that I don't recall seeing a lot of from him. His next pair of dogs did a good job, but they were not Princess, and he treated them so differently; it was sad to see. I think that since he loved Princess and was so hurt by her passing, he guarded himself from even trying to love them. That was difficult to watch; these two dogs just wanted to be loved and taken care of, as we all do.

Jack went and got Red and Frisky a little while after Princess's passing. Red was a reddish-brown pointer. Poor thing, he was very homely, with a short nob tail and skinny body, but he was pure love and went to anyone to receive it. Frisky was your average hunting dog. If I remember correctly, she did the most work between her and Red. Red tried, he really did, and Frisky was a good dog and did a better job than Red and followed Jack's directions to execution just about every time. She had big brown doe eyes and brown-tipped ears, and the rest of her was just soft cream fur. Either way, I remember the way those dogs would light up when they saw Mimi and how she did as well.

Another one of my most favorite memories of your mother was how she would answer this one question when I would go over to her house on any given time, and I would say to her, "Hi, Grandma, how are you today?"

She would always answer with her biggest sweetest smile and say, "Well, I think I am goin' to live. Doesn't that sound nice?"

"Yes, Grandma. I believe it is," I would usually reply.

This exchange would always make me smile or laugh a little. Even when she wasn't at her best, this was always how our conversations began. Even toward the end, when she would repeat herself, or I would get up and return, and she would repeat everything over again. She had dementia, and it was awful. That is gross understatement; however, it is a horrible way to lose someone, to have lost her that way. In the end of her life, there were no stories, no remembering shared experiences; it was just that sinking feeling in my stomach waiting to see how she would react when she saw me. How I would have to explain who I was and see that fear in her eyes because she didn't recall me. If I had to get up and go the bathroom, I was doomed to repeat the whole event again, and it was always horrible. I learned to make sure that when I did need to leave, I made sure to end our visit for that time. I am wondering if she was thinking about you more than she usually did. She might have always been thinking about you. I am sure that you were never too far away from her thoughts.

It is funny going down memory lane with you, especially since you must have had such a different dynamic with her since she was your mother. Subsequently she didn't want us to use her real name; I will use the name she preferred. She would get mad and storm off when she wasn't called Mimi. Especially by family members such as my mother and everyone else that was younger than her. I find it ironic that she would get so dramatically upset if we called her Lena, and she wouldn't do the same for you. I do remember my mom repeating a comment that Jack, her father, would repeat often. He would give a huge sigh, sometimes roll his eyes, and then say, "I love my mother, but I don't care for Lena."

I believe the best way to understand you is to dive into our family, which holds some of the keys to what an extraordinary person you were. It seems that our origins start back in Texas, which is a place that I have never visited. I am a Washingtonian and have *never* stepped foot in Texas. It was not even on my radar as a place to visit; however, now I might have to take a gander.

Mimi, in all her complexity, had a good story behind the name change, and it is due to my Aunt Nita. When my Aunt Nita, my mom's sister, was very young, she was not able to say *Lena*; it came out sounding something like Mimi. Since Nita was her first grandchild, and my great-grandmother was obsessed as grandparents can be about their grandchildren, she loved it and was Mimi and wouldn't be called anything else. I am sure you heard the story. Nita was your first niece from your brother, Jack. I know that Mimi was overjoyed to have her first grandchild, her pride and joy as she would say. She really was overjoyed to have all her grandchildren and great-grandchildren and was a good storyteller, and that is something that I got to grow up knowing and admiring about her. I have lots of wonderful memories of her and the time that we spent together. I remember her telling me about being a very young child riding in the white covered wagons while her family was riding across America to what was called the New World—Texas at that time.

Unfortunately, I only have stories from Mimi's side of the family. Chauncey's side, your father's side, is unknown to me and the rest of our family. Anyone that would have had access to them is long gone now. There is an ancestry account that I can investigate. My aunt started an account a little while ago. I might find more information that way; it is worth a try. One of the many stories that she told me about was her paternal grandfather that fought in the Civil War. She said that he became so angry when he witnessed a Yankee soldier push his mother down because she wasn't willing to give up her last farm animal: a mule. He signed up after that even though he was not of legal age to enlist. He became a scout with a group of people traveling to the New World. After this, he came home and married his sweetheart, and they had two children.

Later, her grandfather returned to Texas and began to set up a home for his young family. She said that her grandmother joined him by train a little while later with one child by hand, another by hold-ing, and one unborn, and that was her father, William Alfred Wagner. According to my great-grandmother, her grandfather had built a home for his family by traveling often to buy lumber, since it was not avail-able where he was planning on building the house. Apparently, he was one of the first to create a home that had wooden floors. In one of the photo albums, she has pictures of the house while she is outside playing with her father. It is amazing that they were able to capture those moments at such an early stage; cameras at this time were only available to upper-middle-class consumers.

As for Mimi's mother's parents, they came from Tennessee to Texas and settled in Grapevine, Texas. This is where Mimi's mother, Ida Roxanna Peters, had their second child. Then they moved to Henrietta, Texas, and settled there for a while. This is also where Mimi's parents were married and where Eugenia Adeline Wagner and Lena Wagner were born. Mimi's birthday is September 25, 1900. She remembered when she was two that they moved to Whitesboro, Texas, where they stayed until she was six. I had forgotten that Mimi and my dad have the same birthday. It has been a long time since we celebrated them together.

Going back to Mimi's father, she thought he was the best! She felt that he was truly one in a million. She spoke often of him. Her repeated description of him was that he was over six feet tall with a gentle soul. She said that she believed that her father built an airplane before the Wright brothers were ever heard of, and when he tried to test it, it was too large to take out of the third-floor attic room where he had assembled it. I didn't find any proof of this story in all the albums, but like I said earlier, she could be a great storyteller at times. This interest would later become one of the strongest bonds and shared interest between him and his first grandson, Jack.

Her father was a licensed and ordained minister for the Presbyterian Church. He had not graduated from high school, college, or even seminary. However, he was ordained under a special clause because of his fine character. When I asked for a little more information, she wouldn't or couldn't elaborate. I know that this is from memory, but it didn't feel right or accurate. I find it very interesting that he was able to be a minister without holding the proper credits; however, there was a shortage of ministers at the time, so I have a feeling that was probably a little more the reason. I could be wrong; it is the impression that I get.

Since this didn't feel accurate, I wanted to investigate the history of the Choctaw Nation and their relationship with the Presbyterian Church. It seems as of lately that every time a story comes out, there is only one perspective getting looked at. For the sake of the Choctaw Nation, I wanted to try to see it from their perspective as well as the Presbyterian Church. I know that my great-grandmother loved living in Texas and Oklahoma and thoroughly enjoyed being at her school; however, I feel that a brief history lesson on the topic is needed.

The Presbyterian Church had kept a presence in the Choctaw Nation with the intent of establishing mission churches and schools (Parker 2017). The Presbyterian Church was the first to faithfully serve the Choctaw people in both Mississippi and in Indian Territory. According to the U.S. News & World Report, the Choctaw Nation is currently the second-largest federally identified tribe in the United States (Rezal 2021). They had their religious texts translated into the Choctaw language, along with all other academic subjects, to help the Choctaw children become familiar in these areas. I found an article by Nakia Parker, who was a doctoral candidate in the Department of History at the University of Texas in Austin. Their mission was closely related to the federal government's forced civilization plan for Native Americans, which included implementing secondary farming practices, unified government, Christianity, and slave owning (Parker 2017). The government wanted the Native Americans to settle down to farm life, then they would stop hunting, and this would lead to Americans having access to the land for themselves. I am sorry for going off on a tangent like that; I like knowing the bigger picture of history.

Now that I have a better understanding of the Choctaw and Presbyterian history, some of what Mimi was saying makes more sense. When she was six in 1906, they moved to Durant, Oklahoma, Choctaw Nation, Indian Territory, where she was terrified by stories that she had heard. However, this was not their experience at all. Mimi recalls the Choctaw people were very friendly and welcomed them. Her family belonged to the Cumberland Presbyterian Church and later became the Southern Presbyterian. Her church provided schools for Native American children, and my great-grandmother went to school along with them. She was there from first grade through high school. Mimi had spent her formative years in a private church for Young Indian Ladies Boarding School. She was a day pupil because they lived near the campus. The president and his wife were close friends of her parents; your grandparents and boys were strictly "off-limits" at the school, so she said she was the designated go-between. She was in a lot of hot water from being in this position a lot of the time. I think secretly that she enjoyed it, but of course, she wouldn't admit it. She liked being the middle of things, that I do remember very much!

While looking through Mimi's 1915 yearbook, I was also curious about the history of this area and building during this time. It turns out that this school started out as the Calvin Institute in 1894. It was grown and renewed as the Durant Presbyterian College in 1896. By 1910, it was expanded again and then called the Oklahoma Presbyterian College for Girls. According to the monthly column in the *Choctaw Nation Newspaper*, Iti Fabvssa, which means "pole" or a "long slender piece of wood" (Iti Fabvssa 2017), the same building is now where Choctaw Nation of Oklahoma headquarters since 1975. The building has now been sited on the National Register of Historic Places in 1976.

While I was reading on the Choctaw writers' column, I saw an interesting story for their reasoning as to why they chose the name Iti Fabvssa. The Choctaw communities keep a record of their history through oral stories that have been passed down from generation to generation. One of the versions of the story goes as such: The Choctaw originally lived far in the west. Life had become extremely tough for the Choctaw and Chickasaw, and they were directed to take a journey together to create a new home. Every night, the prophet placed a blessed pole in the ground, and by morning, a mystic force would have caused it to lean in a direction, and that was the way to travel the next day. Every morning for months, even years from some versions, the pole was found to be leaning to the east, and so they continued. Finally, in what is now Winston County, Mississippi, the pole remained upright all night, indicating that they were home (Iti Fabvssa 2017). That is a beautiful and meaningful reason to honor those that have come before and bring the past to the present.

Bringing that history to the forefront of Mimi's timeline, in 1919 she graduated from high school. Your mother's family moved to Sherman, Texas, where her father was associated with the Texas nursery. She attended Kid Key College for one year and then completed two years at a girls' school in Sherman. Her father wanted her to attend Austin College, a Presbyterian college in Sherman; however, according to her, she wasn't interested in going to a school with boys. It is ironic that she said the previous statement while she was just so sure that her purpose in life was to be a mother. Mimi recalled that when she was six years old, a friend of her father's asked her what she wanted to be when she grew up. Without hesitation, she announced that she was going to get married and have a baby. And she fulfilled that aspiration and then some—she got married and had Jack and then you.

Even though she felt her purpose was to get married and have a baby, it didn't deter her from having a career as well. She truly was motivated and resourceful and didn't seem to let any setbacks slow her down. I found a large black-and-white photo of Mimi sitting at a secretary's desk in a room. The picture was taken from the hallway looking in at her from a side view. She was the secretary president of Austin College from 1947 to 1963. Now I understand why she was so organized when it comes to making lists and putting things together.

From reading all about the different jobs that she had and continued to work when things were down, it is inspirational. She never spoke of Chauncey, her husband, and if I ever asked, she would change the subject or get very quiet, and I could tell that she was thinking but not going to answer further. I think it still hurt her in the end; I am sure it hurt you too. She simply said that they married on November 21, 1923, and that she met him through her sister's husband, Paul. His name was Chauncey Depue Kolb, and they were married shortly after meeting. I could not find any pictures of their wedding together or anything else on the list. It was like it didn't even happen, except for Jack and you. They later divorced, which I know was incredibly painful for the family.

However, she kept on going and went on to alter dresses and worked awhile at the air force base hospital in Sherman, Texas. Jack was in the Air Force so that left her and you to move in with your grandmother. Later, I am thinking because of needing extra income and to help with living expenses, she said that she rented out your house to another couple. That must have been difficult for you.

A soul crushing event happened that shaped Mimi's life and yours as well. In 1937, Mimi's father had to have a hernia operation. He made it through the surgery with no issues, and they were discussing how they were going to get the wheelchair up the steps of their home from the street of the house. When they had him at home, he slumped over in his wheelchair and died. His death was a severe blow to the family, especially Jack and you, his two grandsons. Her mother accepted it and went about adjusting to a life without him. I believe that Mimi never really recovered from the loss of her father; he was her hero. Losing a parent is never easy.

After a string of other jobs and trying to go to school herself, you had to move to Virginia and be away from your mother and father. You moved to Virginia to be with your aunt and her husband. I am not completely clear on all the facts during this time; however, I believe that you were shuffled back and forth between Virginia and Texas. I know that this was a common practice with lots of families to move their children around during trying times. While Mimi tried her hand in different careers that had her moving around the country, that was a lot of huge changes for a middle schooler. How it must have felt to be separated from your parents, even though they were divorced and in different homes and so far away too. Middle school is a very difficult transition period, let alone with all those changes involved as well.

From that whole transition, I was extremely surprised when I found out that Mimi married her second husband in 1969. I vaguely remember him—Lyndon McCutchen. His first wife died in 1968, and they were married the next year. He was a gentleman who was very hard of hearing. I remember his hearing aid would ring all the time, and while visiting with Mimi, she would have to ask him to turn it off or down, and then he couldn't hear anything. He would just read or watch the television while we talked. I figured that they had been married right after her previous marriage ended; however, that was not the case. I don't know how long after they got married that they ended up leaving Texas for Washington State. Mimi had decided to follow her first granddaughter and move over to western Washington, since her oldest son was still living in Richland.

For a short time, Lyndon and Mimi lived on the west side and then moved to Richland, Washington, where they lived right next door to Jack. Growing up myself, it was wonderful to have them next to one another. It was extremely easy to go over for visits, and they were just right there. As an adult, I have a different perspective. It must have been difficult to have your mother and mother-in-law right next door. As wonderful as family is, it can still be difficult. Space is always necessary. You, however, were 2,718 miles away. That is a two-day and fourteen-hour train ride, or if you drove, it would be forty-one hours and nineteen minutes. That is quite the difference in distance between her two sons!

Either way, there was always quite a bit of distance between you and your family. You had your own dreams and knew that they wouldn't be accomplished in the places where your family was located. While you were growing up, I hope you had a good relationship with Aunt Gene and that she was someone that you could confide in and feel safe around. I know that you needed someone, just like the rest of us do. I heard two different stories about the exact reasons why you had to be moved to Virginia. Mimi alleged but didn't explain the seriousness of your asthma issues; nevertheless, she just said that was the reason why. The other reason that I was given is that you were different. You had a different mindset, purpose, or lifestyle is what I remember being told growing up. Getting clarity on the subject was not something that I was able to achieve, and if I asked either Jack or Mimi, they would clam up or change the topic. I believe that given the nature and the unfolding of your death, I would not want to talk much about it either, but I was a kid and asked lots of questions.

However, on April 13, 1979, Mimi received the worst phone call that a parent can ever get—that you had been murdered. Mimi and Lyndon had to get on a plane from Sherman, Texas, to New York City and identify your body. They spoke with the police, and she gave a possible name of who it could have been that did this to you. They were told that it didn't matter and that they would not be going forward with any investigation. The unbelievable amount of restraint, frustration, and anger that she must have had in the situation to begin with, but to be spoken to about her youngest's demise, it is too much for me to even comprehend. It was not your lifestyle that took your life; it was someone else's ignorance and hatred that did. And to this day, they have not been held accountable.

Everyone needs to know that they are loved, safe, and that there is someone here to talk to when they need it. Like I stated in my initial letter to you, I am trying to educate and participate in acts of kindness and support in helping others with issues that are affecting communities in our area and nationwide. For now, I have subscribed to GLAAD, which is an organization that fosters positive media representation of LGBTQ+ people and issues they are facing. It will keep me updated on GLAAD happenings and help me by being more informed. It will also help me see more ways that I can assist others. It isn't much, but I feel that it is a good first step.

In the end, I think that is what we all need to hear and feel. I am left with the feeling that Mimi did the best that she could have. I mean no judgment or criticism of her by my words. I don't think that I could have done what she had to and carried on afterward. It was an amazing amount of strength, courage, and love that she displayed and carried on through the rest of her life. Goodbye for now, and I will send another message soon.

Affectionately yours,
Stephanie

PS—This poem that I found of yours is wonderful. My aunt has the book that you created with a lot more of your poems, and she is working on getting me my own personal copy of it. I can't wait to see them all. I have been a fifth-grade teacher for a while, and I rarely see poems that are written this well or even from this age group. This is one of my favorites. I wonder if this is how you felt about life at times. I can see it. I couldn't have written that well at eleven years old—few can. Your book of poems is filled with the beauty and complexity of a true artist. I am curious, was she supportive of your gifts? Something I guess that I will have to ponder.

A New Snow Fall

Out of the gray winter skies
Sifted tiny flakes of glistening
snow
Trees are covered with cakes of
pearl
With its burden bending low.

The ringing brooks once merry
Are silent, quiet and forlorn.

Hushed in icy Silene.
As a new snow fall is born

—Buddy Kolb
402 Washington Ave
Sherman, Texas (11)

CHAPTER 2

Life Together

Darling Bill,

There were many adorable pictures of you and your brother; however, I think I liked this one the best. It looked like your childhood was wonderful! The smile on Jack's face while he is sitting behind you says it all. Your precious face is too much! The out-pouring of love that you were receiving from immediate and extended family, you both were able to experiment and try to figure out what your interests were. I guess that while Jack was busy with creating and building model airplanes, you were busy creating as well. I can only imagine, as a mother, what watching the two of you must have been like and what messy outcomes became of your adventures.

It looks like Jack and you had a good time growing up in Texas. You both had your own interests that would later help catapult you into your careers. The trials and adventures that you experienced when you were younger helped you both have great perspectives on what you wanted your futures to be. Either way, your brother-to-brother relationship was very special to both of you. I have spent a lot of time looking over all the black-and-white photos of you and Jack. It is so interesting how looking at your young faces, I can see so many of our family members in them. Both of you were such cute babies. I see why Mimi was such a proud mother! It is so funny to see my Grandpa Jack with hair! He didn't have any while I was growing up. I guess having three daughters might do that to a person!

In one of Mimi's stories, she said that you used to take clay from the "walls" that lined the creek that both you and Jack used to play in all the time. Since Jack used the dining room table for his creations, you used the sofa as your studio and a pot for your clay. The creek provided many strange creatures that seemingly took over the house. You learned that polliwogs become frogs, and one time, while Mimi was cleaning the house, she looked at the floor lamp and picked it up, only to find a surprise ant farm in a one-time fishbowl. Other times, she might find a chameleon, alligator, ducks, guinea pigs, white mice, or rabbits crawling along in the house. You had a real animal kingdom going in your home, that is for sure!

When I opened the next photo album, I found an 8×10 black-and-white picture of a cute house. It must have meant a lot to someone since there were several copies, and since I have seen pictures of this house many times before, either you, Jack, or other family members are sitting in front or just posing for the camera. The front door is in the middle of the house, and looking at the house, there is a chimney to the left of the door with two lattice-shuttered windows on both sides of it. On the right side, there is a big bay window with shrubbery all around the front, and to the far right, there is a rounded doorway that leads to the back. On the chimney, there is a large *S* closer to the top, but no house numbers. I tried to look up all the other addresses that have been listed on the back of photos or in the albums and don't have a lot of information to pick up from them. On the back of this picture, it says a name and the last four digits of a phone number. I see that in Mimi's handwriting, it says C. D. Kolb in pencil. Either way, it looks like it was a fun house to live in. I don't know if this home still stands or if anyone is currently living in it, and if they are, I hope they have been making wonderful family memories. I know that some of your memories were there.

At one year of age, you were absolutely running around and trying to catch up to your older brother. It delights me to see you being driven around in a wagon by Jack, wearing a cowboy hat that was way too big for you, and carrying around a large umbrella. There were also a lot of pictures of different dogs that you had while growing up. As I had stated in my earlier letter, I know that my love of dogs comes from this side of my family. I am not sure if these wonderful animals were only your immediate family or if some of them belonged to family members or even neighbors on the same street. I do understand my love for animals from seeing all your pet members, as well as the ones that you brought home to live with you. There are numerous pictures of you and Jack sitting in the lap of a man with a white beard and mustache, light-colored shirt, and pants with suspenders. I believe that it could be your great-grandfather. I mentioned him in one of my other letters as well. It is always nice to be able to put a face on a name, especially when it is family.

As I continue through more pictures, I find you in front of 1920's cars, holding old pigskin footballs, sitting on the porch, lying against the tree in your front lawn, and both of you together in what looks like an old tub. There are some more pictures with the two of you holding tiny puppies and driving around in a metal toy pedal car in overalls in the summertime! So cute! What fun and exciting adventures you two had together!

I enjoyed the pictures of you both with your dad; unfortunately, there are not very many. It does appear to be winter due to your dress attire! All three of you have flatcaps on and are bundled up with gloves and, it looks like, a few layers of sweaters and shirts. In some pictures, I can see the snow, and in others, it looks like ice. You were both trying to make snow angels in a few of them, and you both stopped and looked at the camera to take the picture. In another, I see the two of you hold a sled at different ends, and it looks like you are trying to figure out where you want to go with it. Chauncey is in only two pictures, and in one of them, he is holding one of both of your hands and Jack's in it. I might send a copy of that picture in another letter to you later. You both are smiling, and Chauncey even had a small smile on his face. I hope that your life together was as good as it appears in the picture.

On the next page of the album, I see pictures of just you. In one, you are standing in front of a metal toy airplane pedal car that must have been Jack's. A few others of you standing next to a bike, it looks like the one that I saw Jack riding on a page previously in the album. I wonder if the two of you had paper routes. On the bottom of this page in the album, there is a picture of you in overalls and a hat with a brim of some kind, and underneath the picture Mimi had written October 1, 1929. And underneath that, it says that your tonsils were going to be removed the next day. A sign of many other hospital trips that were looming in your not-so-distant future.

One picture that stands out for many reasons, and I would say is the catalyst for your future and what it held for you, was the large picture in the middle of the page. It is you dressed up as George Washington. You have an uncomfortable-looking wig on with buckles on your shoes, tall white socks up to your knees, a velvet waistcoat, knee britches, a long white shirt with ruffles at the neck and sleeves, and a long colonial jacket. You were the lead of the George Washington play at your school. Theatrical at any age, weren't you? I love it!

There seems to be a little bit of jumping around on your family timeline in this album, and it does jump to the 1930s in the next series of pages, and it appears that you are on a family vacation. There are some pictures of different times together with family members at Lake Dallas, Texas. It looks especially pretty, and you all seemed to have a good time being together and surrounded by nature. Now I understand why Grandpa Jack loved fishing so much and being on the water; it must have brought back lots of wonderful memories of his childhood. Another page says that you were on a Kolb family outing in Sulphur, Oklahoma. The page is filled with pictures of the same waterfall, and everyone is standing at the top of it or sitting in the water as it cascades down to the bottom. Another wonderful family adventure captured!

In a different photo album, it starts off with pictures of Mimi's parents and grandparents. Some pictures are of her when she was little, and then it jumps to sporadic pictures in the 1950s and '60s. Most of the pictures are of you and family members on boats or near water. Either fishing trips or boating fun seems to be how our family liked to spend our free time.

There was another family tradition that started later, I believe. I remember that Jack really enjoyed going hunting. He liked to go feast and duck hunting as well as fishing. I found more pictures in color this time, and there were even pictures of my grandmother going hunting too. She looked happy about it in the pictures, too, but I don't remember her speaking fondly of her hunting experiences. Did you ever visit and go on one of his many hunting trips? I couldn't find any pictures of you in them, but you never know.

In that same album, I found pictures of your visit to Richland, Washington, that I discussed in an earlier letter. My cousins, growing up, were Jack and Mimi too, so a lot of Jacks and Mimis in the photos. There is one picture that stands out for me. It is a picture of you, Jack, and Anita. Anita is in between you and your brother. Both you and Anita have big smiles on your faces and are looking right at the camera. It is a nice picture of the two of you. Jack, however, is looking to the side, as if he is talking to someone else. It reminds me of a conversation that I had with Anita, my grandmother, when I was younger.

She said that she knew who you were back then and that she was fine with it. I know that now, that statement is not a true sign of openness, but it was how she felt. She said that she always had the best times when you were around. You were so fun and friendly. You look happy to be around her as well.

Was she someone that you could confide in and that was supportive? I personally feel like we would have talked for hours if we had been given the chance. Going back to your George Washington play when you were little, was that your first play? You knew that you were supposed to be destined for more, for better. It is ironic that George Washington was possibly your first play and how the name is more of a foreshadowing for your future. I know that you know what I mean. There will be more to come. Be on the lookout for another letter shortly.

Love always,
Stephanie

PS—In my continued attempts to do acts of kindness and support in helping others and to become a better ally to the LGBTQ+ communities, I tried to expand my horizons today, and I chose to follow a group on social media. They are called NBJC, or National Black Justice Coalition, and they are a civil rights establishment that centers on encouraging Black LGBTQ+/SGL people and their families (NBJC 2021). They post about upcoming events, ways to help protect and respect people in their communities, and tell people's stories. It will continue to keep me informed on current issues and allow me the opportunity to help in other ways.

PPS—I thought that since your childhood was spent in Texas, you would appreciate this poem you created about Texas.

Hurrah, Hurrah, for Texas

Hurrah, hurrah, and double
hurrah!
The day of Texas has come, has
come
The flute and the fife are playing
And I'm with the huge bass
drum, bass drum.

My folks do you see what I'm carrying with
It couldn't take long to guess, to
guess,
For I am carrying the Texas Flag!
So beautifully it is dressed, is
dressed.

Hurrah, hurrah, and double
hurrah!
Come and cheer my Texas Dear
Let us be happy on this good day
Hear them cheer, let us cheer too.

Hurrah, hurrah, and double
hurrah,
The day of Texas has come.

—Wm. C. Kolb

CHAPTER 3

Jack Kolb

Beloved Bill,

This picture of your brother, Jack, my grandfather, makes me smile so much. I cannot get over how young and happy he looks. I understand that he is carefree in this picture, but it shows a time when he was being his own person and exploring the possibilities of his life. There were times when I would see this similar look on his face, but they were short-lived and not very often. It makes me kind of sad when I think about it. How life can beat us up instead of always trying to find gratitude in it. Easier said than done for some folks, I guess. He went through a lot of traumatic events, and so maybe he couldn't see it. He did have a lot to be grateful for, and I am hoping that he found peace with life in the end. This was when he was a cadet, and surrounded by this picture in the photo album that I found it in, there are several others of him dressed up in Air Force uniform. It is amazing to see these pictures of both your lives and try to put the puzzles together. It was probably hard for him to leave you.

I know that you both cherished your relationship. You were each other's best buds, no pun intended. You played together for hours and were inseparable. I am so grateful that Mimi took such good care of all the albums and that family members continued that tradition after she was gone. I was able to see the love and admiration that you both had for one another. You can tell how proud she was of her boys and family through the photo albums. From what I have gathered, you two were so different. Jack was left-brained, and you were right-brained. I guess opposites attract, don't they?

My mom, Patsy, helped me find a few more photo albums that have helped me piece more information together. Since Mimi lived next to Jack, when she died, all her stuff was taken over to Jack and Anita's home. Then Jack got sick, and Anita couldn't take care of him; she had a difficult time taking care of herself, so he had to go into an assisted living facility. He hated it. I remember him saying in the beginning of his stay at the assisted living facility that this place was going to destroy him. To see the change in a man that was such a force of nature go to not having a say in his situation was devastating. He, very slowly, deteriorated, first physically, and then mentally, right in front of us.

His speech left him not long after being there. It was so difficult to understand him, and it only strengthened the frustration that he had when he tried to tell us something. He knew that he was saying something, but it came out in cries and moans. He was a prisoner in his own body, and when I start to think about how he had to go down that scary and angry road of what life was like for him, I don't want to imagine it; it hurts too much. He was such an intelligent, proud, and perplexed individual. To see him like that was one of the worst memories that I have.

He stayed there for approximately two years, and I always wondered if he thought about you during this time. I can't imagine the places that the mind goes when alone and stuck somewhere that you don't want to be. Mental health issues, regardless of the time, should be taken with care. I know that my grandmother did the best that she could, but I still wish it could have gone differently. Don't we all when it comes to family and close friends? He was officially labeled as an Alzheimer's patient, his mother, Mimi, having been diagnosed with dementia.

There are seven stages of the disease, and around this time, he was in between stages 4 and 5. Stage 4 is mild Alzheimer's and just needs some assistance to stage 5's needing 24-7 care. His depth perception was off, and that caused him to have falls and injuries that my grandmother, who had had two knee surgeries, was unable to help with. She had to make the decision after a particular incident where he had fallen and hurt himself during the nighttime, very badly, and there was no one at the house to help get him up. So an ambulance had to be called to get him the help that he needed. It left him in a bad physical condition so that there was no other choice but to have him go into a facility that could provide these services for him. It was a horrible way to watch someone that you love fade away slowly and observe as pieces of them go missing that will never be connected again. For all the tragedies that he suffered in his life, this was not what I wanted for him. This is not something that I want for anyone. I keep going back to the same thought: If you were there, would things have been different?

As mentioned earlier, Mimi wanted to be married and a mother. You were her second, and Jack, my grandfather, was her first. Jack Wagner Kolb was born on September 30, 1924. The name Jack came from a neighbor's baby that Mimi had cared for and carried around on her hip when she was only six years old. She loved the name so much that she named her firstborn after him. The name Wagner was Mimi's maiden name. Jack was the pride and joy of her family.

When I spoke with some family members, there was one story that struck me as so funny, but in a nutshell, it describes exactly who my grandfather was. I believe you both were still in younger adolescence then. There were snakes where you lived. You painted a beautiful painting of that time together when you were young boys, playing in the close-by river, and there were many, many snakes, not to the liking of Mimi and other family members.

Anyway, I believe you both would catch them and bring them back to the house. Mimi and her sister would occasionally find them while cleaning the house. Both women started wearing gloves whenever it came time to cleaning. Something else happened after you both had discovered snakes. Jack had been capturing them, and then Mimi noticed that he started wearing snakeskin belts. He had figured out on his own how to turn snakes and their skin into belts. My grandfather has always been someone that tinkers with things—engineer, even at a young age. Once an engineer, always an engineer. Just as you knew that you were going to New York City!

Another adolescent story that Mimi told me about Jack growing up was the airplane kit that he received. Your aunt gave him the kit, and he assembled it and launched it into flight. After that, he was hooked on putting together model airplanes and even started designing and building them on his own. He flew them in competitions. In the old family photo albums, there were several pictures of Jack putting this model together, getting it into position to take flight, and then more of them in flight. He ended up asking for only mothballs and castor oil—that was fuel for his airplanes—and nothing else for Christmas. He seemed to turn the entire house for his airplane creations, so much so that dining and mealtime became standing-room only. From what I remember of my grandfather, this seems right on target.

On the bottom of some other pictures of Jack, Mimi wrote that he and someone named Bryan went on a trip to South Texas, the Valley, and Mexico. There are several pictures of him at Randolph Air Force Base in Texas, as well as a couple of him in front of the Alamo. I wonder if this is where he got the inspiration to become a pilot and go into the Air Force, or if he already had it in mind, and this made that decision that much easier. They are beautiful pictures of the area. He traveled to a lot of places, but he never talked much about it with me growing up. I would have loved to hear his side of the adventures he had.

At sixteen years old, he graduated from high school and then entered Texas A&M College. This didn't surprise me at all; he was a very intelligent man. Due to being at college at such a young age, the hazing that he was subject to cost him a trip to the hospital, where he was subject to severe pneumonia. You had to go with your grandmother after Mimi received the call from one of Jack's friends. They called her, and she left as soon as she could to go be with him. Your father came as well, and then he took him home to recover from his injuries. After he was feeling better, he returned to college and stayed until he could enlist in the Air Force.

Jack became a pilot and second lieutenant in the Air Force during World War II. Near the end of the war, Jack was transferred to an airfield in Madison, Missouri, where he gave flying instructions to other cadets. This is where he met and married my grandmother Anita Walkonis. Mimi had joined them in Madison for the wedding and welcomed her to the family. I laughed at this a little, because those two did not have the best relationship, to say it mildly. Mimi, I think, was just used to being the woman in charge and had a difficult time letting someone else enter the picture. Later, he transferred back to an airfield in Texas and had their first daughter, Anita Louise. After he had served his time, he returned to college to complete a creative engineering program with a select group by General Electric in Schenectady, New York. When he finished the program, he had another daughter, my mother, Patsy Gene.

I know that Jack and Anita had some bad times, just as all couples do. Having children is difficult, and I know that those kinds of life events were not talked about then and just as difficult to talk about now. Something terribly sad happened to Jack and Anita in between the births of Anita Louise and Patsy Gene. They had a baby boy, and his name was Jack. There were only a few pictures of him in one of the photo albums, along with a clipping from the newspaper about his death. Jack W. Kolb II was only nine months old when he died at his parents' home. He was born on June 16, 1947. He was laid to rest in Sherman, Texas. That isn't something that a lot of people come back from, and it was a large strain on their marriage that was felt even in their later years. My mother was born four years after Jack was gone. Bill, did you get to meet him?

After this, they left New York and moved to Richland, Washington, where he was able to use his creative abilities to help design and perfect the Test Facility Reactor in the Nuclear Program. The Hanford Site is in the southeastern part of Washington, next to the Columbia River. The land was originally inhabited by Native Americans, such as the Wanapum Band, Yakama, Nez Perce, Umatilla, Walla Walla, and Cayuse Tribes. Other parts of the land were settled by non-Native Americans as well for the sake of irrigated orchards, farms, and ranches before World War II (EPA 2023). It was a 586-square-mile region that was used in 1943 for the creation of plutonium for nuclear weapons. This comes from the Treaty of 1855, where five thousand Native American chiefs and tribal delegates met with Washington's and Oregon's territory governors to cede 60,000 square miles to the United States government in exchange for the Yakama Nation Reservation in Washington, the Umatilla Reservation in Oregon, and the Nez Perce Reservation in Idaho (EPA 2023). From this treaty agreement, the land was to be handed over to the government to produce plutonium, and then it was taken to New Mexico for the final step. Jack was asked if nuclear energy was dangerous, and he gave a resounding "It is dangerous as hell." This is why there was such careful and exact attention given to every phase of its design and operation. For his work, Jack and his teammates were given a certificate of achievement by the president of Westinghouse Hanford Company. Around this time is when they welcomed another daughter.

To balance out his strong focused career, he was an avid hunter and fisherman. He also did some wood and metal workshops where he invented, designed, and converted his boat into a cart with retractable wheels that could be tucked up on the sides of the boat when he went fishing. I got to see his hunting and fishing prizes that he would bring back. They had big freezers that they would stuff with his trophies. I remember the giant fish that he had mounted on the wall over his fireplace. I also remember when someone in the family bought him one of those fish that are mounted on a plaque that would move its head and sing. He laughed like a kid with that gift. He kept it close to one that he caught.

Mimi had said that he created objects with wood and metal; however, I didn't get to see many of his creations. I would have loved to see him create something. I do remember that he would go to his workshop and tinker but never came out with anything. When I was little, I was disappointed. I would have loved to see him be creative or invent something. I wish that he would have let me see a little of the real him. He was so guarded and aloof; I thought that was just him. I think that truly, he missed you very much.

On a rare occasion, I do remember going fishing with him. It didn't happen very often, and I don't remember it being that much fun, but I did get to see this creative side. My brother and I had our lines out, just waiting for something to bite somewhere along the Columbia River in Washington. Jack had already had a few bites but decided not to keep anything that he caught. It was toward the end of our outing, and I finally got a pull on my line. I was so excited; I couldn't believe that I was finally getting my chance. When I pulled it out of the water, my excitement changed to shock and terror. This thing looked like it belonged in a horror film; its lips were bigger than the rest of its full little body. It was close to four inches long in total, and its lips were massive. I just remember laughing hysterically, and seeing Jack laugh at it as well was something that I didn't experience much.

Anita used to go on fishing trips with Jack, but for some reason, she had stopped going. My grandparents had a long marriage, about sixty-two years. I know that not all those years were happy. It was obvious at times that it was quite strained, but that is a very long time to be together with someone. I remember when I was younger, we celebrated one of their anniversaries with a big family reunion. I think someone put on a slideshow with all kinds of black-

and-white photos and pictures of all our family. One of the songs that was playing was one of Grandma's favorite, and they both got up and danced together. And after they danced, they held each other's hands and just smiled and looked at everyone together. They were enjoying the creation of this family that they had started a long time ago, and all the bad times were erased, and the magic of that moment will live forever in their hearts. I wish so much that you could have been there.

I had a preconceived notion of my grandfather through my experiences of growing up around him. Now I realize that it was such a narrow perspective, and I have such a better understanding of why he was the way that he was. I grew up knowing that your brother, my grandfather, was a very knowledge-able, resourceful, and methodical individual. He did exactly what he wanted and, on his terms, his way only. He was unapologetically himself. He could be kind; however, if you disagreed with him, he wanted evidence to back up your side of the conversation and was relentless in his opposition.

He believed what he believed and was prepared to argue to the end. I just thought that was who he was, that he had always been that way. It was fool-ish of me to think that. No one becomes that rigid without life kicking you along the way. I know that life was hard for you, too, Bill, and in many different ways. But I now realize just how hard it was for Jack as well. I am so grateful for the time that I had with him and even now when I look back and realize that there was so much more to him than I had thought. I appreciate that time even more; he was doing the best that he could. Like the rest of us, hanging on and knowing that our best doesn't look the same every day.

There has always been one aspect of Jack and Mimi's relationship that has always stumped me. You ought to know better than anyone else. What happened in their relationship that made things so tense and complicated? Like I have said earlier, Jack was not an easy man to do anything with. He was closed off, and it took a lot to get him to even smile or laugh. The reason that I say you would know better than anyone is when I look at two pictures. It must have been some military gathering that you all went to together, I am not sure. In one picture, you are with Mimi, and you both look so happy and carefree. You have your arm around her, and both of you are smiling ear to ear. She couldn't be happier or prouder of you if she tried.

However, in the second picture, it is Jack and Mimi. Jack is dressed in his cadet uniform and has his hat on, but there is absolutely no smile on his face. He looks miserable by all definitions. Mimi is sitting right next to him but not leaning in and barely smiling herself. She is posed, but clearly something is off. There is no arm around her in welcoming. It looks like someone forced them to take a picture. Is this the time that it started to change between them, or had it been like this for a while? I remember him always having an icy demeanor, and I never could understand why. I don't mean for this to sound like I am judging them, just trying to understand where things went wrong and why. It only got worse after you were gone. Their relationship was their relationship, not for me or anyone else to understand. And even if I did know, it doesn't mean that I would get it. They had a complicated past.

One person that I know missed you very much was Anita. My grandmother Anita told me a lot about you. She loved you to pieces. She thought you were one of the funniest, most creative, and sweetest people that she had ever met. She said that she knew who you were the whole time. She said this was more likely the reason you didn't feel as welcome to come to visit, and that is why you stayed away. You were being disrespected by your own family, and I can't imagine how much that must have hurt you and that you had to carry that terrible pain around.

Due to the heartache that you carried around with you, I took another action step to help and support in becoming a better ally and signed up to have the newsletter and follow them on social media; it is called the Trevor Project. This program's mission is to end suicide among LGBTQ+ young people (Trevor Project 2023). The Trevor Project is the world's largest crisis intervention institute for LGBTQ+ young people that are under twenty-five years old. The more information or resources that I encounter, the more likely that I can help. Every young person needs to know that someone else loves them and that they are needed. It is just that not every young person knows this or has access to people that can give them that message. They can receive help any time through multiple ways. It truly is a wonderful organization. I know you had your own hardships, setbacks, and secrets too. I am sure you would reach out and help in any way that you could as well!

Thinking of you,
Stephanie

PS—After I finished this letter, I found another photo album with pictures of you holding all three of your nieces. In each picture, you look so lovingly at them. The one with Nita, I can see the dimple in your left cheek from a big smile that you were giving her. You are wearing a checkered shirt and sitting in front of a windowsill. She was the first, so it was an amazing time. You have the same smile on your face as you were holding my mother. That big dimple shining through as well! They were in Schenectady, so it was closer and easier to see them. I couldn't find the picture of you with the youngest daughter; it was taken out of the album. I just found the writing underneath where the picture had been. I am so happy that I was able to see more pictures of you with your family.

PPS—On a sidenote, did you know that your brother was a *Star Wars* and *Star Trek* fan? Jack associated all his commentary with verses from the Bible, and when he asked for the trilogy of the first three movies, I was so shocked. When he watched any one of them, he acted like a little kid again. The first one came out in 1977. Did you happen to see it? It is a huge deal now; he would have loved it! In lieu of that, here is one of your poems about the moon since I couldn't find any of your poems about space.

The Moon

Oh moon that grows so round
and bright,
Moon that flows around at night,
Oh moon that goes and slips,
And sails around like a dream
ship.

—W. C. Kolb

CHAPTER 4

Bill Kolb

Darling Bill,

This is another one of my favorite pictures of you in your uniform. It is such a handsome picture of you. You look so happy and proud of what you were able to accomplish. After being rejected from all the other armed forces, you were admitted into the United States Army. There is another picture of you and your brother together dressed in uniform—I can't find the original of it. You are on the left, and Jack is on the right, both so handsome and have the biggest smiles on your faces.

You were born on June 4, 1926. June is a big birthday month for our family. My brother and my twin daughters were born in the month of June as well. My girls would have loved you! All of this makes me think about how things were for you growing up. "Little Buddy" was the nickname given to you by your brother right off the bat to learn and explore this world with. Jack and you were very involved in different types of games and interests growing up. It looks as though Mimi dressed you both alike most of the time. There could be lots of various reasons why that is, but I did notice that from the photo albums and that you seemed very happy and at peace as a young child.

Another thing that stuck me was that as a kid, you really were sick! While I was looking through some of the photo albums and mementos from our family that my mom is letting me borrow, I came across a scrapbook filled with get-well cards, letters, messages, and telegraphs from loved ones over the years. It seems that there have been many ailments in your life. I am not sure when it started, but it seems like you were very sick with asthma in your earlier years. You were in the hospital numerous times.

While reading through the scrapbook, I found a lot of get-well notes that family and friends had sent you. I also learned that you had to have your appendix removed. There was an interesting card that had an operation questionnaire in it for the patient, you, to fill out. The first question was the ABCs of how you were prepared for your operation. It went on to ask if you were sore or not, any dreams, how long was the incision, what kind of stitching, and even a temperature checklist. There was even a blank person so you could draw exactly where you were operated on. It is difficult to tell which cards are for the asthma hospital trips or the appendix removal ones. Either way, you made it through all of that.

It seems that during these multiple hospital and doctor visits, Mimi perfected her taking notes and making lists back from her days of being a secretary for most of her professional career. I remember when I would visit her, she would have these different notepads in leather covers, and she would have all kinds of notes in them. They would always have rubber bands wrapped around them to close them due to their alarming volume. I don't remember what they were about, but I know that they were superimportant to her. She had them in baskets all around her official chair that she was always sitting in. This was probably a coping skill that she used when you were in the hospital, and she diligently made notes on who gave gifts at the hospital, donated food, gave of their time, and then had a star system on how she had given thanks to everyone that had decided to help. Whether it was a letter, speaking to them in person, or sending them something in return as a thank you. Unfortunately, she had lots of experience since she had to do this several times when you were younger and then again later when you were laid to rest.

Looking at your timeline, you graduated from Sherman High School in 1944 and were a graduate from Austin College in 1948. I am looking at your high school report cards right now. It looks like during your senior year, you were in speech, trigonometry, civics, and typing. You did extremely well in speech, trigonometry, and civics. You didn't do as well in typing, not your thing. I get it, not mine either. You scored the best grades in speech. Again this doesn't surprise me since you were so theatrical. Not me, I would get tongue-tied, and my neck would get all red and splotchy. I would stammer and struggle just to get to the end. I hated it. However, with students, I don't feel this way. It is funny, I have no problem standing up and talking with a bunch of students; however, put me in front of a bunch of adults, and it is a different story.

While continuing to look through family photo albums, I found a program for a play at Sherman High School in 1943 that you were involved in. It stated that the senior class of Sherman High School presents; however, you were not a senior until the next year. Anyway, you were the lead in the play, George McIntyre. This play was originally performed in the Ambassador Theater in New York City; it ran from November 23, 1933, to December 6, 1933. It was a three-scene play that was taking place in the McIntyre residence in a university town in Northern California. You had almost the whole cast sign your program; I think that is sweet. I love the picture that was inside of the program, too, only six of the cast on stage, and you are holding what looks like a baseball bat and looking at the cast member who is holding a ukulele. Everyone looks so young and carefree, as seniors usually do. They were ready to head off to the next step of life. Continuing the topic of plays that you were involved in on November 1–3, 1945, you were cast as Oliver Bashforth in theater associates presents *The Enchanted Cottage*. In the movie with the same name in 1945 as well, the character that you were playing was named Oliver Bradford, not Bashforth. You were the lead in the play! That is wonderful!

A year after graduating from high school in 1945, you were a camp counselor and at the Richmond Professional Institute, College of William and Mary, performing in the theater. Since you were a camp counselor, I believe that you did this before the play in 1945. Mimi kept a postcard that you sent from New York on June 23, 1945. It has a picture of the Statue of Liberty, and on the card, you start off saying that you are at the foot of it. You wanted to let your family know that you were having a wonderful time and that you would be leaving in the morning and that you were trying to see as much of the city as possible before heading out the next day. The postcard ended saying that you would write again at camp.

The other piece that I found was the Buzz Book Camp Sheldrake handbook. It lists all the camp counselors and campers. As a teacher now, it is kind of scary that it lists everyone's address in it. But again, it was 1945, not 2023. That would not happen today. As I was looking through it, I noticed that in the back, there is a space where you can write things down, or it is called last-minute flashes. And it is blank except for the name Paul Robison/Robinson written in pencil. I looked through the names to see if he was a counselor or camper, and there was no Paul listed with that last name. And there are other Robinsons listed in the book, but not with the first name of Paul. I am curious as to who this person was for you.

There were other achievements that you had, I heard stories from my mom and aunts. You even helped with building and designing that stage setup and backgrounds as well in the play. Even though the pictures are in black and white, I can still see lots of detail. There is a beautiful pattern that looks like it could be the wallpaper for the room in the cottage. Also, there are painted furniture, mirrors, painted cracks in the wood of the walls that don't have wallpaper, and a painting that is hanging by a string on the wall. It looks like the door was even painted to look like a wood door and boarders for the door. In these pictures, you are dressed in a three-piece penguin tailcoat tuxedo and have a costume parted pencil mustache on. You have a very serious look on your face as you and all other members on stage are staring at a young woman who appears to be writing on something while sitting down in a chair. It looks as though everyone on stage is waiting to hear what she has to say next. In another picture, it looks like there are beautiful portraits painted in elegant frames. I know that had to be you—painting portraits was one of your specialties!

Now that I understand the premise of the play, there is more to see in another picture; it looks like it could be a different scene in the play. You are stage right and speaking with the person who is playing your mother. The both of you are standing in front of a desk and talking to each other. On stage left, there is a younger woman watching the two of you during your discussion, standing behind a couch that has an older man who appears to be blind, sitting quietly on the couch. In the background, I am not sure if it is painted or if there really is another room, perhaps a foyer with stairs.

In the program, it is stated that the scene is laid at a cottage on the edge of Fittlehurst Park. There are three acts in the play: Act 1 is the relics of war, Act 2 is the strange happenings and a dream, and Act 3 is the eternal truth. Also in the same program, it looks like you wrote "Trippy" next to one of the other actors in the play. After your disappointment with no longer being in the army, a year later, you were playing a wounded war veteran who ran away from his fiancée and mother to only fall in love with another woman in an enchanted honeymoon cottage. What a way to take your broken heart and make it better! You took all that energy and harnessed it into something different, better, and moved on from it. I am so proud of you! Not everyone is able to take a misstep and turn it into something wonderful and creative!

I imagine that you were able to use your experiences both good and bad to help you in your performances. Since you were finally allowed to join in the infantry, where you heroically tried to be a soldier. I am looking at the pictures of you in uniform. The pictures were taken in Richmond, so you must have been standing in front of your Aunt Gene's brick house. There is a cute little girl in a couple of the pictures with you. She looks like she is proud of you. You look so happy and ready to take on anything. I know you were proud of yourself, as you should be. However, on November 21, 1944, you were discharged after just a few short months because your asthma took control, and it devastated you. I know that after being let go, you returned to Richmond and went back to college. Your asthma has been the hot button for a lot of issues in your life. I was able to look at your discharge papers, and they did say that you were of excellent character.

The bandwidth of expertise with which you were able to use left and right brain capacities is truly incredible! You graduated in May of 1948 with a bachelor of arts degree in biology and chemistry from Austin College with honors and was very involved in the performing arts. While you were in Richmond, you studied fine arts and dramatics at William and Mary from 1943 to 1946 before returning to Austin College. You even attended the University of Texas Medical School from 1948 to 1949 before deciding that it wasn't a good fit for you or that something else was on the horizon.

On August 4, 1945, you received a letter from the Plymouth Drama Festival at the Gateway of Cape Cod, at the Priscilla Beach Theatre in Plymouth, Massachusetts. It stated that you were invited to be a part of the festival's thirty-first session that was set to begin June 19, 1946. You received an appointment certificate as well with the letter. It stated that all 1946 candidates were invited and that you were fortunate to be part of that group! I was curious if this was still an active festival, and it is! It is now called the Priscilla Beach Theatre, and I am following them on social media. It was established by Dr. Frank Trask in 1937; it is an original barn summer stock theater. There have been several generations of actors that have experienced this festival, such as Paul Newman, Pat Carroll, Sandy Dennis, Jean Seberg, Albert Brooks, Rob Reiner, Kitty Winn, Peter Gallagher, and Jennifer Coolidge. I am in shock right now; this is amazing news for you!

There was even an article written about this festival and how transcendent it was becoming for young actors in America. It was written by Robert L. Wheeler from the *Boston Globe* in the *Parade Magazine* in 1945, where he stated, "*Priscilla Beach gets the cream of the young acting talent in America… Applicants are carefully winnowed to keep out young-sters who have no serious bent for the stage. It has to be a good, rugged ego that survives the course in theatrical realities offered by Dr. Trask and a faculty of 14 instruc-*

tors and directors." He also stated that "*a nationally known institution systemically shopped by talent scouts*" (Priscilla Beach Theatre 2023). Technically this was the year right before you had been asked to join, but c'mon, this is incredible! I mean Paul Newman was a student in 1948, two years after you!

You had been chosen from several hundred applicants from every state in the country. The evaluations were based on the dramatic backgrounds, personal confirmations, and transcripts of record. Candidates who qualified are wanting to work in professional theater or radio or even weekly productions in theater. There were talent scouts at this festival, and in past years, many had gone on to Broadway, radio engagements, and serious acting careers! While this festival was going on, there were four Broadway plays opening at the same time, to be followed by new productions each week. This was right up your alley! The four Broadway plays were *Hamlet*, June 3, 1946; *Second Best Bed*, June 3, 1946; *The Dancer*, June 5, 1946; and *Icetime*, June 20, 1946. Did you audition for anything? Help with production? I wish I could find out more information regarding your involvement in this festival. I hope that you had the most wonderful time!

I am completely blown away by this experience you had! Unfortunately, there were no pictures or stories that were told to us. My biggest take from your Plymouth Festival experience is that I have way more questions than before. For some actors, this was their breakthrough experience that led to much more success. For you, however, when it came to acting, it just stopped. There is no mention of any other performances or plays; it just stopped. If you went through this amazing experience that very few individuals get the opportunity to take, why did it stop? I am left to assume that it had to do with your "lifestyle." This makes me incredibly angry at the thought; however, I am uncertain of the true reason at this point. When I looked up how actors were treated when it came to LGBTQ+ individuals in the 1940s and 1950s, it was awful. They were persecuted for being themselves and were even given clauses that had to be signed to keep them in check, and if they didn't follow the rules, there were severe consequences. They could be arrested and lose their careers. There were concessions with the police department and the paparazzi if they broke rules and steps that were taken to destroy those that didn't comply. Is that why you didn't actively participate in any more plays or productions? Was that dream taken away from you too? You typically played the lead in any production that you were in, so like I stated earlier, I am only left to guess.

It is unclear if you didn't share or if you shared with Mimi, and she didn't share with us. Either way, this was a huge step in the right direction for you, if performing was what you truly wanted to do with your life. That was in 1946, and then there is nothing in the photo albums until 1955, when you brought someone with you to Mimi's house. There are four different pictures that I am looking at, and I have a lot of questions. I know that Mimi didn't like to share you or your brother, especially with another woman. She would still make it known that she didn't care for them or would be off-putting. I know that my grandmother Anita experienced that from her a lot being married to Jack. You never married; however, you were involved, possibly engaged. I heard different versions of the story, so I will just have to go with what I remember being told. The first of the four pictures are charming with you, Yvonne—that was her name—and another couple. All of you have the biggest smiles and are crammed together at a table in a restaurant or bar for everyone to be the picture. It looks like what a selfie is now. Don't worry, I will explain about it later.

In the next picture, it is you and I believe the girl from the couple in the first one. She is smiling brightly, and you look happy but are looking off to the side. I can see a can at the table with a white-and-red checkered tablecloth. I must assume it is red and white since the picture is in black and white. The third picture is of the man and Yvonne. She is holding out a drink to him, and they are both smiling and laughing, while he seems to be pointing at something. It looks like you all are having a very fun night.

The last picture is the one that sticks out the most for me. Yvonne must be the one taking the picture because she is not in it. Anyway, it is you, the man, and the other woman squished together. I wish that I knew his name; however, he has squeezed in between you and the other woman. They are smiling very big and bright, just like in all the other pictures. However, you have a much different look on your face. His face is right next to yours, and you have your eyes closed, as if you are trying to savor the moment and lock it away in your memory.

You have a soft, subtle smile that leads me to think that he meant something to you. I could be wrong; it could just be a flash moment that you closed your eyes. You could have had too much to drink, and that moment was just captured. I am thinking of so many other reasons why that look was on your face. But I can tell you one thing: in all the other pictures that I see you and Yvonne in, none of them have that blissful look on your face. I don't believe in coincidences either; he was extremely pho-togenic. He looks like he had a cheerful and fun-loving personality as well with big bright eyes, expressive face, and dimples. In the end, I have no idea. I don't know how you met, when, or even what his name is.

Yvonne was a very pretty woman, and I know what I said about Mimi not liking to share you with others. However, she looks kind of happy to be standing next to her. Yvonne doesn't look that happy to be in the picture with her, though. I do like the picture of you and Yvonne on the couch, holding each other's hands. It is a nice picture, but things work out the way that they are supposed to. She was meant to go a different path than you. I hope that you both were able to stay friends afterward.

I thought you might want to know what happened to her. If I found the correct person, she lived to almost ninety years old. She graduated with a teaching degree—yeah! Like me! She went to Saudi Araba to teach, got married, and had children. It sounds like she lived a wonderful, fulfilling life. Good for her! She was a very stunning woman, and it looks like she had a wonderful life, and isn't that what we all want!

For you, your escape, passion, or inspiration for life was the arts! It has been the whole of your existence, and you knew that from day one! The life that you wanted to have been filled with all kinds of art and experiences helped shape who you were. Another unknown quote that I found really resonates with your life, "Humans are obsessed with escapism—through movies, books, music, art, daydreams. Our souls really weren't made for this world." How true that statement is! With all your creating a different world, it must have helped you live in this one, especially with all the highs and lows. I am wondering if there was any celebration of your life in New York. I don't know. I wish that I could find out. Through the course of your acting journey, life could have been so different for you. There could have been other opportunities in your life, but due to certain circumstances, there weren't, and it makes me so angry to know that you kept being set aside, or your dreams were crushed.

In my voyage to help others in your name's sake, I joined an organization today in my continued search for better knowledge and being an ally to those in need of the LGBTQ+ communities; it is called GLSEN. Their mission is to make sure that all members in a school community are respected and appreciated regardless of orientation (GLSEN 2023). I am sure that you would agree and be supportive too! I will send you another message soon.

Love always,
Stephanie

PS—Here is another poem of yours that I enjoyed.

THE WIND OF SPRING

Hear the wind moan,
Ho-o-o-o-o-o-o-o
The prettiest sight and sound,
If you could only hear it too.

Hear it call the birds to halt,
See it rock the trees,
Hear the tulips say,
Don't you wish you were me.

Then it whirls the kites in space,
Going in leaps and loops,
Oh! Wind please don't go,
And then it comes back in troops.

—Wm. C. Kolb

CHAPTER 5

Major Change in Family

Hello Bill,

Here is the picture that I mentioned in an earlier letter to you, and there are not many pictures
of Jack, Chauncey, and you. If I had to guess, the
family dynamic started to come apart, and this led

to making an impression on you both for the rest of your lives. Which one of you looked more like your father, you or Jack? When I get really close to the few pictures that there are of him, I can see both you and Jack in his face. I tried my best to find more pictures of your father. I was unable to find Chauncey and Mimi's wedding pictures or even their wedding certificate. I guess that Mimi wanted everything gone, so she got rid of it all! I am sure that she either got rid of them, or someone else in the family might have them. Even looking through all the albums decades later, she tried her best to erase him from her life. I am trying to see it from her perspective; it is painful to end a marriage and completely change what you thought your life was going to be like. Not just a unique way but a completely new way of thinking going forward in life. She had to think of her kids and herself and how she was going to move beyond her circumstances.

She had to be incredibly strong to pick up the pieces and create a new life for herself and you during this time. The divorce rate in the 1940s was incredibly low at this time. It was unheard of to divorce but possible. There are many reasons why it ended, but it was their decision. Of course, when there are children involved, it makes it more difficult. Either way, it is heartbreaking that everyone had to endure this event.

I know that your parents' divorce was devastating and emotional. Their marriage started to fall apart in 1940, and they divorced two years later.

My understanding of the situation that unfolded was your father had an affair with someone that he worked with or that came in to his place of business. After your mother found out about the situation, she was either unable to or did not want to forgive him. She made a swift decision that she thought was best. I wonder, if they had stayed together and tried to work it out, would everything be different? Would you still be here? It is silly to ask such questions, but it is something that I ponder now and again. The marriage was terminated on May 21, 1942, in the District Court of Grayson County, Texas. You would have been around sixteen years old at this time. That must have been difficult for you.

During my childhood, I didn't hear a lot about Chauncey. I do remember that if the conversation ever drifted to Chauncey—and it would very sparingly—usually Jack would bring it up, and Mimi would huff and puff about the topic, and Jack would try to get his point across; however, Mimi would not have it. Like I said, it didn't happen often, but on the occasions it did, it would be a little elevated. There would be slightly raised voices, and both would try to get their own point across without listening to the other. Every family is different when it comes to communication; everyone wants to say their part, but not everyone will listen. I remember, as a little kid, sometimes feeling very uncomfortable when those kinds of conversations have been had right in front of us. I look back on it now as lessons on how to be better when there are times of adversity or indifference. I am sure that you had many conversations like these with both.

Anyway, I liked his name. Chauncey D. Kolb was born in Sherman, Grayson County, Texas, on August 30, 1894. He was six years older than your mother, Mimi. He was born and raised in Sherman all his life and died there. I know that they met through her sister—your aunt—and her husband. I wonder if there are still Kolb members in Sherman, Texas. Unfortunately, that is about the extent of my knowledge of your father's side of the family. There had to be other cousins that you played with or grew up with that could give me more insight, right? It seems sad that that is all I could find. I might have to investigate some kind of ancestry website and see what connections that I can make. I would have liked to hear more on his family's side of events or, quite honestly, anything to do with our family at this point.

I did find out a few pieces of information about your dad's side: Chauncey and Doris were married from June 5, 1951, until Chauncey passed away on October 2, 1966. They had no children from their marriage together. I know that Jack would go over and visit when he was home, and I am certain that you did as well. I know that Mimi didn't want to know about anything that happened after you had gone to visit him. I guess I can understand that, but it must have been difficult to transition back and forth between two homes, then not being able to share any experiences with her. Both of your options sound very unhealthy and too much for a young adult to maneuver in their own hurt and needing to feel safe.

The effects of divorce are difficult for a child, but for a teenager, it can be even worse. A teenager, due to their more mature stature, will be given more responsibility, and this can cause other negative ways of coping. Teenagers will be handed more chores to complete since there is one less person in the household, or a parent will inappropriately vent to them. Teenagers are not ready for the responsibility of picking up where a parent left off, and since everyone makes mistakes, it is quite possible that you could have had this happen to you with your mother or father. You were not emotionally ready to deal with the absence of your father from your home or the extra responsibility that his presence left behind. Maybe moving to Virginia was a good escape from what was happening at home.

This is when major changes started happening. Your dad moved out, and Jack wasn't there but at school, so it was just you and your mother. Then the costs of the family started adding up, and you both moved in with your grandmother. After all these extreme changes, it was decided that you were going to move to Virginia and live with your aunt and uncle for a lengthy period. I know the main reason for your moving was due to your horrible asthma. At first, I thought that this was cruel and unnecessary. However, my brother grew up in a desertlike area such as Sherman, Texas, must have been, and he had horrible asthma as well. As soon as he moved to the other side of the state, to the Seattle area, his asthma was gone. Still, I understand doing whatever you have to for your children to feel better and to be able to survive. I don't think that I could move one of my children away from me.

I thought that with this letter, I would want to focus my acts of kindness and support in your name and find a support group that geared itself toward LGBTQ+ children of divorce or separation. It is called Rainbow Families, and it is monthly, virtual, and focused on peer-focused support to its diverse community in all forms. It can be utilized by divorced and/or separated families and helps create a secure and relaxed atmosphere for families to tell their stories and help one another. I will receive information through email and on social media about events, and there are special activities available for families to try (Rainbow Families 2022). It seems like a wonderful organization that is doing great work for families. I keep going back to the same questions: Would this have been something that you would have wanted to be a part of? I truly believe that even if you were not involved as a young person, as an adult, you would have wanted to get involved and help. That is one of the reasons that I feel called to help in this matter, in your name.

Did you have friends in both areas that you could feel safe with? Peers are one of the most important parts of a teenager's life, and not being with their friends would be the end of the world. I hope you did have friends that you were close to. Did you tell any of them about your dreams of going to New York someday? I hope you know how much, this time, speaking to you means to me, since you can't respond back. I understand that it is one-sided, but a part of me hopes that you can hear. We will speak more later.

Sincerely yours,
Stephanie

PS—I have noticed that your poetry is mostly focused on nature. That must come from all the time that you spent on family vacations and maybe just your free time in nature.

A CALL IN THE WOOD

Listen to the call in the wood,
The cardinal is singing,
And her young is cooing,
And the brook is softly ringing.

Sh! Hush the bluebirds are greeting,
Look at the woodpecker's bright red hood,
While the lark is answering,
To the Call in the Wood.

Look, the sun is going down,
The mocker to his mate is singing,

And yonder in the greenwood
tree,
The chickadee's voice is joyously
ringing.

Now it is dark and all is quiet,
They are getting ready for another
busy day,
The babies are nestling under
warm breasts,
They think the call has gone to
stay.

But they are wrong, indeed they
are,
For it will be there in a short
time,
It will be as gay as ever before,
And out of their nests the birds
will go.

The day has begun, the sun is up,
The wood call has already begun,
All the birds are as busy as can be,
And the trees are singing to the
sun.

—Wm. C. Kolb

CHAPTER 6

Bill's Illnesses

Bill,

I am wondering how you are feeling after my last letter. I know that divorce is such a large and encompassing topic, and I wanted to make sure that it is okay to continue. Going from divorce to your illnesses is not necessarily a step in a more fruitful place; however, it is another huge subject that I wanted to discuss with you. You were such an ill child. From severe asthma and appendix removal as child to the other dependence issues as an adult. After some of the stories I heard, it would make sense to venture that you experienced depression throughout your life as well. I mean being in and out of hospitals in your childhood, experiencing the divorce of your parents, having to move back and forth between Texas and Virginia, being let go from the army, and many other things, too, that would have been a lot to take. That is life; nonetheless, we all need reasons to feel better and to move forward. Unfortunately, we sometimes find those answers in the wrong solutions.

Turning to alcohol could be due to several different reasons, one that I know of: it does run in our family. I don't know the specifics nor do I need to. It is something that you grew up seeing from your dad and maybe other family members as well. I believe that you had a long history of depression, alcoholism, and drug abuse. I don't mean for that to sound like anything more than just a statement. Just love and understanding what it was like for you and how that directly affected your life. Now I believe that I understand where the desire came from to enter medical school after you graduated with a liberal arts and biology and chemistry degree in 1948. You must have wanted to help others and yourself, and this was the way that you thought it would be possible. I do wonder why you didn't finish. I am sure you made the right decision for yourself at that time.

Was there such a stark difference between both sides of your family? What little I did know about

Chauncey was that he did drink extensively, and that shaped your young mind too. I know that Mimi didn't. Coming from a strong Presbyterian upbringing and her parents being so close, and from what I gathered, there was not any or very little drinking on her side of the family. That could have been confusing as well. It can be extremely difficult growing up and seeing those different philosophies playing out in your own family, if that was the case. And especially after the divorce, the sides were chosen, and you were given two completely distinct models of what families can look like. I believe that it can add to an already heavy or stressful existence while trying to figure out your place in this world.

There was this paper that I found in the old binder of your Wilbur sketches (they are so cute by the way). I noticed that you wrote when you must have been in your physiology class while you were attending medical school. The topic of choice was related to the conditioned reflex in the treatment of chronic alcoholism. It is very clinically written, and you received an excellent score on it from your professor. When you are heavily invested in the topic, especially in the cases of your own family, it can help strengthen the focus and intent of the message. I keep thinking if you were trying to help yourself from falling into this trap or if you were already in it and looking for a way out. I know how personal this topic was for you.

You used the results from a survey of 3,125 patients that were admitted to the Shadel Sanitorium in Seattle, Washington, from the years 1935–1945. It was stated in the research that in most known cases, it proves that this conditioning therapy, when properly implemented, is one of the most successful and most economical of methods for treating chronic alcoholism. It is now one heated way of helping addicts and in short-term results; however, long-term, it has unclear results.

In your paper, you also used cited information from Pavlov and Voegtlin to discuss the techniques that were used. However, it just seemed to boil down to abusive patterns being used to "help" patients. Abusive measures can't be used for long-term results, but you were careful and covered your bases with your paper. When I was younger, I didn't look at your paper because I didn't really understand; I just enjoyed looking at the characters that you drew.

Alcoholism and addiction became a big part of your life as you got older. Your choices became more erratic, and you ended up needing extra financial help from Mimi through those uncertain times. I can imagine how difficult those times were for you; it is never easy going through them or even having to ask for help. Asking for help can be one of the most heart-wrenching things to do, but sometimes it is necessary, and when we do, it is fortunate to have someone that can respond and assist. I know that you had a lot of different jobs. Sometimes getting work could be challenging, and I am sure that New York City was expensive too. That, along with the mental struggle of trying to become an artist in a city full of other artists and not finding adequate success, well, I think that would cause me to rethink things or to possible rely on something else that could give me a brief escape from that all-consuming feeling.

I know that all these issues became overwhelming for you, and you asked for help. Mimi helped you out as much as she could, and it became a burden on her financially also. Unfortunately, she saw a pattern and decided to take you out of her will due to your financial woes. She was worried that you would just spend it all, and there would be no one to take care of you. I don't know that that was the best decision to make, and it seems cruel. I am not sure how she justified this decision with you, but that is none of my business. We don't know the future, and she was a planner and level-headed thinker, so she must have made the best decision that she thought she could. I know that she thoroughly enjoyed being with you on her trips to New York but knew that it was coming at a cost to both of you. A lot of this doesn't seem to add up for me. I know that there are pieces of information that I am missing; you probably know what they are. It comes across as painful intentions for you overall.

Was being taken out of the will an issue that caused a rift between brothers? Or was there a distance between the two of you due to something else? I remember my grandmother saying many times that you two were not close as adults. Your visits became fewer and fewer, but there could be financial reasons for that. I have heard other family members say that you might not have felt very welcome coming home. That breaks my heart, substantially. Why would you want to come home to see family if there were only triggers waiting for you? I wouldn't either. I would have made my visits as few as possible too, but there were other family members that really did want to see you, so you made your way. I know that my aunts were happy to have had you in their lives. My cousins that were older than me remember you, and they were happy to see and visit you too. I am so sorry, there was not more time to get to know them.

You must have felt that you wanted a change in your life, so you started the process of rehab. Not sure when and where; those details are not available to me. After all of this, you joined a program and were able to stop drinking. That is truly amazing! I am so proud of all that hard work that you put into your decision to stop. And I am sure that the hard work continued both during and after. I am sure that it was not easy, and it was something that you always had to work on. Some days were better than others, but it was a choice, and you made it. That is what made your death all that more upsetting. You worked through your childhood trauma, your illnesses, and adult traumas, too, only to have someone end your life. I am looking at your death certificate again. We never got a reason why either. Mimi and Lyndon were told that due to your "lifestyle" choices, they would never find out who did this to you.

In the 1970s, New York City was a complete mess. I know that New York City was better at having a more positive attitude toward LGBTQ+ communities, but people were still criminalized for it. And there was the significant increase in all crime, the recession, the music industry moving to California, Son of Sam, a major blackout that caused chaos and looting, and hiring freeze. That is more than enough to send a city into ruin. Still during that time, there were so many wonderful things that kept the city going. I haven't been to New York City yet, but one thing I do know is that I have always thought of it as one of the hearts of art in our country and a place that I want to visit very much. With all the darkness that happened, there was light that came through in the form of art: novels, paintings, galleries, and movies; they all came to life to inspire as only true artists can do. I would like to think that we all enjoy a good comeback, especially when it is still an era that is talked about to this very day. Bill, I get it. I completely understand why you decided to stay and be a part of something that is so unique, utterly beautiful, and diverse. You wanted to be a part of something special and knew you were supposed to be there. I just wish that I could have visited you there instead of this.

However, the response that Mimi received from officers should not have been the end result. Really, lifestyle choices? You were a talented artist who was loved very much by your family. Didn't we deserve the right to know who did this? You knew the person, you let them in, and they stabbed you multiple times and possibly stole art. There was no pending any further investigation, just that you was gone. I was told that some of your art was taken, but there is no record and no one looked for that. I am sure that someone else must have seen this person leave, but no one came forward. I don't know if questions were asked or if they moved on to the next one. I know that Mimi gave the name of someone to an officer, but nothing became of that inquiry. I am so angry, this is unacceptable, and your case sits somewhere in a storage facility. How many others have suffered this same feeling or situation, only to be told that nothing can be done about it? There are works of art out there somewhere that we have never seen. I wonder if anyone else were to find these letters and know who I am talking about. I have wanted to go and open the cold case so badly; however, other things have taken priority. I am hoping that one day soon, I can. We might not get any answers, but it is better than not trying. At least I can say that I did.

Love always,
Stephanie

PS—I wanted to act in your name, and I thought that it should be centered around alcoholism and/or support groups. Since I know that this was important to you, I figured I would look and see what ways I could be supportive to others. I found the American Addiction Centers, and it has information, facts, treatment options, and statistics that are geared toward the LGBTQ+ communities. Since substance and addiction rates tend to be higher in LGBTQ+

communities, there should be facilities and services that can be customized to the special challenges that they face. It is always best when seeking help to find those that understand what you are going through. On the website, there is a number, live chat, and a link for those that are willing and able to check into a facility for help. I know that you found a facility that worked for you, and I am so proud of the strength and perseverance you showed in our own process.

PPS—Here is a picture of your Wilbur character that I grew up looking at every time I would go over to Grandma Mimi's house. I would spend my time reading about these characters that you created and loved so much!

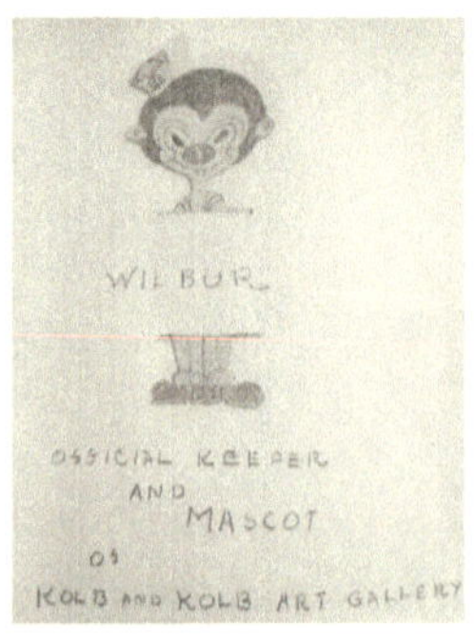

CHAPTER 7

Discovery/Life in New York

To my Great-Uncle Bill,

Here is a picture of you and Mimi in front of your apartment in New York City. The address was 227 Waverly Place, and I looked up this location today, and it looks very pretty. The building is beautiful, and it looks like it was and is still a great place to live in. I can see why you enjoyed it so much. Waverly Place is a northern boundary of Washington Square Park and is known as "the Row," and it is owned and used by New York University. The street would later be made famous by a novel, a Disney show, a television series, and a famous zombie movie. You knew how special this place was and its proximity to all kinds of venues that were associated with the life and career that you wanted to have. I keep wondering what you would have been able to accomplish if your life had gone in a different direction.

I am not sure of the date of the picture; however, you look very tan and a little too thin. You have a cigarette in your hand and wear no smile. Mimi had to stand on a step to be similar in height to you in the picture. I am short like her, so I understand. She looks pleased to be there with you. The picture is taken too far away to really see your face. That might have been on purpose. I know that she enjoyed her trips to see you very much. Apparently, she would come back and share with everyone all the fun, sights, and sounds that you would take her to during those visits. I know that you were very busy with multiple projects at a time. From painting portraits to the planetarium, store window dressings, and more, you had many aspiring jobs that helped you pay for and maintain your life in New York from 1950 to 1979. My aunt was looking through her stuff for her own wedding picture and came across a copy of your résumé, and then she sent me a picture. I am so grateful; this helps me out with some of the holes that I have had in discovering your life.

Waverly Place is still the address listed on the top of your résumé. In your summary of qualifications, you stated your experience as a designer of display items, such as props, backgrounds, and illustrator of these artifacts, an experienced painter in oil of commissioned portraits, both in formal and informal settings and age groups. The last item I had no clue about was your experience as a general clerk in the Department of Building and the Department of Parks, Recreation, and Cultural Affairs for the City of New York. You dabbled in everything! This piece of information gives me a little more insight as to what your timeline looked like.

In your detailed work experience, the first job you listed was at the Hayden Planetarium at the American Museum of Natural History. You were employed there from January 1951 to July 1953 as an associate art director. Collaborating in the creation of special effects for the sky shows in the planetarium, as well as meteorological phenomena reproduced by the slide projection and film, were the duties that you oversaw during your employment. There are some wonderful pictures of you getting ready to paint a mural and working with someone named Mr. Favreau creating a rocket with a lighting system inside of it. The first picture, Mr. Favreau is holding part of the rocket that you are putting together, and on the back of the picture, it says not for reproduction and then lists the Department of Education, the American

Museum of Natural History, and the address. In the second-largest picture, you are on your knees in front of a blank canvas or mural of sorts and have something in your hand that I can't quite figure out what it is. The last three pictures are of the rocket and some kind of display that is set at the bottom and inside the rocket. There is a picture of you holding it before it is set inside the rocket.

Upon closer inspection, it looks like it is a model of the booster rockets that catapult it into space. The final picture shows just how big the rocket size is: it is just shy of your full height. You are getting ready to put the top of the rocket on, or cockpit, and I notice that you look focused but not necessarily happy about what you are doing. Difficult to say; however, I took the picture out of the four little corner pockets that keeps it in the book, and I saw something. Of course, it does say not for reproduction; however, you wrote on the back of this one. It says, "I really felt like this too—Sad, isn't it." There is also a capital letter *A* with a circle around it, and it says same depth as *B*, with a circle around it too. You have added some measurements to the back as well, possibly for future reference. I am so glad that I took the picture out and looked at the back; it confirmed what I had been thinking. Hopefully, you made peace with the outcome and moved on.

The second job that was listed on your résumé was freelance and regular employment with some major display houses in New York. There were six different listings that you worked with from 1953 to

1974. They were Resident Display, Sylvor Display, Timely Services Inc., Decorative Plant Inc., Spaeth Display, and Imperial Display Corporation. I was curious to see if any of these display houses were still in business and the last two on the list were the only ones operating. No one had mentioned any of this to me earlier. At the major display houses in New York, you did freelance work with inventing, designing, and interpreting presentation sketches, merchandising props, and decorative displays for all major department stores and chain stores and creating decor for store windows, both interior and exterior.

While you were employed with the display houses, this is also when you composed portrait paintings. From 1953 to 1974, I knew that you had several portraits in many different states and countries; however, I didn't know that it was extended into other countries as well. The beauty of your work is incredible and unlike anything that I have been close to completing myself. One of the first of the few articles that I could find was written about you returning home to paint a portrait of a sixteen-month-old little girl. I couldn't find where it was published from; however, the author's name was Bill Reed, and from the way it was written, it must have been for a local Sherman city paper.

When you had started the painting, she was not able to walk. However, since you take your time and are very precise, it ended up taking several more weeks than planned due to her mobility progress. In the article, it stated that you ended up having to run around after her to get the portrait complete. I know that typically it can take eight to ten sittings, depending on the availability of the subjects in the painting and their staying power. However, once she learned to walk, all bets were off, and she even started getting into painting and tried to paint on her own. I am sure that you had your own comments or remarks about that experience.

Another story that went around our family was that you painted a portrait of Princess Grace Kelly before she became a princess. I remember hearing about this from several family members, but there was never any evidence that it occurred, so I figured it was false. I am trying to figure out how that could have even happened, you never know. I don't mean to sound negative, but proof would be nice. While looking through other photo albums that were focused on your art, I found out that you painted one of her sisters, not sure if it was Margaret or Elizabeth Kelly, but it was not Grace. Either way, that sounds like an extremely important job that you were a part of, and I am sure that it was as beautiful as could be. It is nice to know that that part of history is in some way true to what I had been told.

There are two self-portraits that I know about; there could have been more. One of them is in my mom's home. It is unfinished. I remember looking at it the first time and just bewildered that it wasn't complete. You just stopped. There are clouds in the sky behind you and some kind of beige background behind you as well. I believe you were looking straight into a mirror while painting this on the last day that you were working on it; you just didn't want to finish. You had told someone that you were very unhappy with yourself and didn't care to finish it. You didn't want to look at yourself anymore. What you must have been feeling that day to make you stop, I can't imagine. As a young kid looking at the picture, I couldn't understand why you wouldn't complete such a beautiful portrait. There was only a small section of your arm and chest not painted in. As an adult, I now understand why this was an option for you.

The second portrait that I didn't know about until I was looking at these photo albums was a completed one, with you sitting in an old wooden rocking chair, looking over the side at whomever looks at it. You look extremely thin and frail in the portrait with no warmth on your face. You appear to be wearing jeans or dark pants of some kind and a black T-shirt. It looks as if someone just asked you a question, and you turned around to answer the person but deep in thought about something else. It must have been one that you painted when you lived in Richmond, Virginia. It is hanging over the fireplace in what I think is Aunt Gene's home.

In another picture that was probably taken at the same time, Mimi is in the photo, standing next to the painting on the wall and holding Puddin', Aunt Gene's Siamese cat, in her arms. She looks very happy and is speaking to someone else that is not in the picture. I wish I knew who has this painting. I didn't know of its existence until recently. It does make me think that there are probably several other paintings or works of art that you created that none of your family got to see.

Looking at all the family dynamics, with divorce, depression, alcoholism, and your struggles with being unhealthy at such a young age, it was inevitable that there would be a trauma response to everything that happened to you. I keep marveling at the factor that you endured all these struggles and still were able to overcome. Like I have said before, it was amazing and nothing short of a miracle. Some people never get back up, but you did. I will say it again and always, I am so proud of what you overcame in your life.

I am sure that a lot of the stresses in your adult life and living in New York City just compounded the issues that you were struggling with. I am left to assume since I haven't been there, that will put extra pressure on a person that is not in Sherman, Texas. The atmospheres are on different ends of the spectrum. There are so many more people that have just as much, if not more, going for themselves as you did. You must prove yourself more, give more attention, create more, create better, keep going. As an artist, I am sure that that pressure could crush most people, if not help cause a reason to dull the senses as well as create an escape from it. There is no link between artists and addiction; it has to do with genetic makeup, childhood trauma, and dysregulated stress system that can cause individuals to be more prone to addiction (Giordano 2021).

There is a notebook of all your doodles that I have had for a long time. It is a unique creation of Wilbur, the official keeper and mascot of the Kolb and Kolb Art Gallery (that was the official title you labeled it!). I have lovingly taken good care of it. Since I was little, it was my favorite thing to look at when I went over to Mimi's house. She loved sharing the book with me and loved my interest in it. She didn't speak too much about you when we looked at it; it always seemed to make her a little sad. However, she loved me and wanted to indulge me in the opportunity to look at it repeatedly. I am so grateful to her for that now. She must have gone down memory lane every time we looked at it, and she kept it to herself so that I could enjoy that time. I wish that she could have told me more about you as I was growing up. It doesn't feel the same looking through old articles, photo albums, and other items to try and put your life together.

There was another job listed that I had no clue about in your life. From 1972 to 1974, you worked for the city of New York as a general clerk in the Department of Buildings and the Department of Parks, Recreation, and Cultural Affairs. I guess you did possess the same set of skills as your mother and harnessed them to work for the city of New York. You were responsible for changes of ownership of management and the demolition of all multiple dwellings in the Borough of Manhattan, New York, as well as clerical work for the Parks Department and assigning welfare recipients and filing their personnel data and payroll. There was a lot of diversity in the jobs and positions that you had throughout your life. I noticed that everything seems to end in the year 1974, so that makes me wonder if you were creating this résumé for the next job.

Regarding your artwork, I was told by my aunt that there is a very strong possibility that there are other works of art you created out in the world. When you were sometimes down and out or in between possible pay periods, you would create a piece of art, sell it, and then use that money however you saw fit. There are many reasons that you could have used the money, and none are my business. I was hoping that if these letters were to be seen by someone who had a work of art that you created, I could somehow find and see it. It is a long shot, but miracles do happen.

There is another organization that I felt compelled to become a part of for your name's sake. I was scrolling on social media and came across a video of a young woman deeply upset and crying because she had the courage to come out to her parents. The strength that it takes for a person—any person—to do this is incredible. Her family's reaction was not supportive at all, and she was devastated. Love is not conditional; it is open and honest. After the video showed her, it transitioned to an organization that helps kids in need. It is called Stand in Pride, and I signed up to be a stand-in family member to someone that needs it. You can text, call, or even stand in a family situation that a parent is missing in, such as a graduation or wedding. As a parent, the thought of not being there for my own children, I can't wrap my brain around it. However, this is one way that I can help someone else in need, just like I think you would have done.

I thought about you the whole time, and I guess I did it for both of us. I don't know if I will get the opportunity to even speak to someone, but I put myself out there. If I get to talk to anyone, I will let you know. Of course not about the details, but you know what I mean. I have lots of love to give, so I should give it, right?

As always,
Stephanie

PS—Here is another one of your short and cute little poems that I thought was worth sharing.

A PARTNERSHIP

A cow, a hen, and a little gray
mouse,
Once all lived together in a little
green house,
The hen built the fire, the mouse
    cooked the dinner,
And the cow, she was a very great
spinner.

They lived together, for many a
year,
So they got up early, when the
sun did appear,
The cow, a spinning, the mouse
asleep,
So the hen of course, had to tend
the sheep.

The day was done, the wind was
cool,
It was the very day to go to the
pool,
So off they set, off on a run,
With cake and jam and a bit of
bun.

The mouse fell in, the hen went
after,
And the cow fell in, in a burst of
laughter,
And when they were in, they
rocked to and fro,
And how they got out, I do not
know.

—Wm. C. Kolb

CHAPTER 8

Bill's Ending

My dearest Bill,

I believe this may be my final letter to you. After saying this, I am incredibly saddened. Our journey together is not over, not by a long shot, but I have really come to enjoy and look forward to these brief little moments where I feel that I am speaking with you. Even though it is not a back-and-forth conversation, it has created a space in my heart that feels like we have a connection that was not there before the letters. In all honesty, there may be some letters that I will send in the future, I just don't know. This letter is the most difficult to write, and I guess that is why I put it off until the end, because it is about your end, your death.

I feel as if I am almost done with the puzzle that I started, but it isn't quite coming together as I had hoped. There are so many unanswered questions, so many gaping holes, I guess only time will fill in what is meant to be answered. Originally, I didn't think that everything was going to just fall into place; still, I do have some clarity and some questions answered. I would have liked to have more; however, that hasn't come to be at this time. Glancing over your death certificate one more time, I found a few things that I had missed earlier. On the line that says usual occupation, it says medical technician at NYC Health Labs. I was stunned that I hadn't seen that previously. Looking up the NYC Health Labs, there are currently several locations, and I looked up the closest one to your apartment. There is one located a little over two miles away. I tried to find out which locations were open back then; however, I have not been able to find the answer to that question. So you were using that year of medical school that you took in Galveston after all. Good for you!

Going back to the other piece of information that I found after another look at the certificate was the address at the top. Originally, I thought it was the morgue or hospital that you had been taken to after being discovered. It was not. It was the address of the George Washington Hotel in New York City. I found a blank postcard of this hotel and didn't think anything further about it until now. I figured that you had given this postcard to Mimi as a souvenir or a place of reference for her to stay when she came to visit you. Maybe you stayed at this hotel when you first arrived and were trying to figure out where you were going to plant roots and grow in the city. Either way, the irony isn't lost on me; this is where your life in New York City began and ended. The post-card has a beautiful picture of the outside of the hotel all lit up at night, and it states that it is in fashion-able Gramercy Park and with the address and phone number on the bottom. When I flipped it over, it also says that the establishment has six hundred modern outside rooms, each with private bath and radio, tele-vision, and air-conditioning, with a coffee shop and cocktail lounge. George Washington has had a theme in your life, hasn't he? It was your first big role that you played, the hotel that you visited and gave a post-card to Mimi, and it was where were you were killed.

It's a hotel, why would I want to stop and dis-cuss this now? Well, I was told by all my family mem-bers that you was killed in your home. I think that that was not the case. Your home in Waverly Place is only 1.3 miles away from this hotel. Did you live in Waverly Place first and then move? Was it due to the financial or physical setbacks that you were hav-ing? Since there is no postage on the postcard, I am not able to put those pieces together. Hotels are usually not homes, right? I looked up the address—23 Lexington Avenue, Corner Twenty-Third Street, New York City—and sure enough, there it was. All these years later, it is still a hotel. So I started to look more into the hotel and see if there might be more answers that I could find.

The George Washington Hotel was first established in 1928 and has a very interesting history. It was later turned into apartments and dorm rooms. Before it was turned into apartments, it had been used as a brothel and bootlegging house during Prohibition. In the 1980s, it was raided by the police and then put up for auction. From auction, it was purchased and became housing for the performing art schools nearby and for paying tenants as well. Then later it was renovated into the Freehand Hotel, which it still is today. While looking at pictures of it now, it is beautiful. Well, I didn't find any answers about you, but at least I now have the correct address for the Cold Case Foundation, if they choose to take the case and help.

Going back to the picture that I sent with my letter, I have to say, this is my favorite picture of you. So young, handsome, and full of life in this picture. The world was just waiting to see what you were going to become, just as all young people that get to start their adult life. You look healthy and maybe the happiest that I have seen in all your pictures, except when you were a child. And you look as though you have come out the other side of the pain and grief in your life and made it your own. That is the funny thing about pictures—there are a thousand words, a snapshot in time, or a stopping of the clock to capture that moment forever.

However, this was the start of your young adult life, its ups and downs, and everything in between. Even with all that hope for the future, you could have had so many different thoughts behind those eyes. You never truly know what goes on in someone else's mind, even if they share it with you. I couldn't find the date of when the picture was taken; however, it is a moment in time that was saved, and I am so happy for it. You went through so many life-threatening scenarios and survived only to get to this point. I know that this picture is prior to all your adult challenges, and in that moment, you were truly content and happy in your life.

I know that living in New York was inspired by some innate force beyond you because it was where you were supposed to be. I have mixed feelings about this since it was also where your life ended. I realize that you were doing exactly what you were supposed to be doing, what you were meant to be doing, but it still doesn't take the sting out of your death. Since Mimi was such a good secretary, I can see all the receipts and correspondence together while she was arranging your funeral. It is weird to look at all of this. The death certificates, the letters from funeral homes, correspondence to the funeral homes for helping arrange all the last details so that they could bring your body back home and celebrate the life you had. I mean, that is what it will all boil down to for all of us. It is so daunting and emotional to be going through the process of these tasks that lead up to a final goodbye. I was alive while this all happened but too little to understand. My parents didn't go since they had both Ben and me to take care of and probably didn't have the means to fly all of us to Texas. I wouldn't have understood any of this anyways being so young. I have cried many times while writing my letters to you. You should have had more time. This was not fair.

I am extremely sad that you are buried so far away. I would like to visit your headstone; unfortunately, that is not something that I have the means myself to do yet. Mimi did have an extra copy of the receipt for your headstone. She bought you a gray granite headstone and had the following engraved on it:

William Chauncey Kolb
June 4, 1926 – April 13, 1979

I am sorry, that is just not long enough. I wished she would have had something else written on it for you. I am sure she wanted to, but maybe she wasn't sure what to say or afraid that what she would say wouldn't come close to how she felt. A parent having to bury their child, there are no words to accurately describe it.

Trying my best to put the events of your death in some kind of order that I can make sense of what actually happened. There was a knock at the door, and you went to answer it. You must have known the person, and it can't be told whether you liked them or not; however, you let them into your room. Maybe the two of you had a conversation about something, and it got elevated in anger or disagreement. There could have been a previous some sort of disagreement or dislike for this person, and they snapped, and the rage took over. Maybe you thought you could keep it from escalating, so you let them in and tried to reason with them. I keep creating scenario after scenario as to what the reason might have been. In the end, it doesn't matter. This person was the last person on earth to speak to you.

Did your life flash before your eyes, like we see in movies, books, or TV shows? I understand that no one can tell us; we will just experience it for ourselves when it is time. I keep thinking about what must have been going on through your mind when this happened. You survived childhood traumas such as illnesses and divorce, being moved to different parts of the country due to financial or other reasons, not being listened to about your name, getting into the armed forces just to be let go of a few short months later, a broken engagement, and going from school to school.

After going through the process of being in a legendary acting festival, and all of your acting dreams just stopped, working multiple jobs just to make ends meet, starting medical school and then ending after one year, being told that you couldn't be your true self time after time, going through the awful stages of drinking yourself into stupors and then magically going to rehab to be free of your substance abuse unlike your father, being bullied because you were yourself, and it made others mad because they didn't have the emotional intelligence you did. Is that what you saw, felt, and experienced with each stab of the blade that was in this person's hand as they ended your beautiful, traumatic life? Did you envision scenarios of your life while they brutally stabbed the life out of you? Pictures of your childhood entered your mind—*stab*—your parents' divorce—*stab*—not being an actor because clearly you were meant to be—*stab*—all the work that you did to get sober and save yourself from dying a long painful death due to cirrhosis of the liver—*stab*. You knew you were dying and that no one was coming to help you. My soul aches for you and what you must have gone through. I can't imagine that someone would do this to you, to anyone for that fact. It is so difficult to write this. I can't stop crying.

They stabbed you several times in the chest, lungs, abdomen, liver, back, right kidney, renal artery, and mesocolon, then you hemorrhaged and died. Just like that. I know that you feared someone, and Mimi had given the officers a name. When speaking with my aunt, she remembered that you told her somebody named "Big Jim" wanted to hurt you badly. I don't know why they disliked you enough to do this, and I will never understand it. Unfortunately, the more that I think about it, they probably didn't think about the guilt, the pain of others, or anything other than themselves.

Since your father passed away earlier, I hope he was there with you. I am so sorry that you were alone and that no one could save you. As I said in an earlier letter, your mother and her husband went to verify that it was you. They never got over it or the fact that they honestly lost you at all. Your body was sent to Texas, where you were laid to rest in Sherman, Texas. The place that you first considered your home but left for so many different reasons.

When I think of the premeditation that was involved in your death, the way Mimi and Lyndon were dismissed by police, and the actual event that happened, I am shaking so badly right now. It is difficult to express my sorrow, contempt, frustration, and outrage. As much as I can understand the era and the problems of the city, I don't comprehend the dismissiveness of what happened to you. You died on Friday, April 13, 1979. You were murdered in a hotel room. With the brutality of your wounds, they had been thinking about this for a while or were just a monster or both. It was personal, and no one paid the price for taking you away from us. No one. It has been in a box or file as a cold case since 1979.

There must be more answers out there for you, for all of us. Understanding that not all stories get the closure that they should and this is part of life. I will continue to look for answers and be open to the possibility that this might be it. I will continue to reach out to others that are in need to the best of my ability, and I will stay current with the organizations, newsletters, and other venues that I have connected with and be present and open. I will make sure to help those that have ever felt how so many feels now, left out, humiliated, cast aside, etc., I will make sure that I am there to let someone else know they are cared for, heard, and seen.

I found an organization that might help me discover more than I am able to on my own. There is one that I found that will provide services to victims or families of victims. They are called Cold Case Foundation and offer their services at no cost, which I think is wonderful. They do take donations, and you must fill out an application first. I am filling one out for you. I have no idea how long it will take. If there is a wait, which I am sure that there is, I will be patient and move forward with whatever information that I am given in return. Trying not to get my hopes up, but I am hopeful. I think we should always be.

There is another organization that I started following to provide acts of kindness and support to others in the LGBTQ+ community. They are called Remembering a Life, and they assist the LGBTQ+ community in the realm of grieving. They help aid with the process of grieving an individual through loss, love, and pride (Remembering a Life 2023). They are accessible through all major social media outlets and have a wonderful website full of extremely helpful tips for those going through a loss and steps on how to successfully honor the person lost. Everyone needs help, and this organization does a wonderful job helping those in need.

Previously, I had envisioned myself as an ally to the LGBTQ+ community. I still have a lot to learn, and I am willing to continue the work to help and become an even stronger ally than before. Getting to know you and how you have helped me in my journey thus far, however, now I must do it on my own. You will always be with me, in my thoughts, and one of many reasons that I keep trying to be better, live a better example of what love really is. I will tell your stories to anyone that asks and will listen to others that have stories of their loved ones that they are willing to share. I will always be hopeful that more answers will come in and that justice will be done for you. And I will hope that for others that have suffered similar experiences within their own family, that they are able to find peace, hope, and justice in their own passages as well. We need to walk forward in love and understanding for all, just as we would want for ourselves.

Love without conditions is the purest
form of love. (Unknown)

My love always, until me meet,
Stephanie

TO WRAP THINGS
UP (SORT OF)

I will continue my mission to push to get your case opened and have them at least review the information and see what is possible. I understand that that might not be possible, and I am okay with it if so. I need to try my best so that I can at least say I did. If a private investigator is possible as well, then I will do that too. Telling your story will be another way that I am able to learn more about myself and help others.

Upon starting this message yesterday, I had stopped after the first paragraph. Later the next day, I received a message from the wonderful people at Cold Case Foundation, and they have asked for additional information to help with the possible opening and investigating further into our case. I am grateful for the opportunity, and I will stand in hope that something or someone will be able to shed some light on what happened. I understand that it can go one of two ways; however, it could happen in our favor, and I am willing to take the chance.

I have no affiliation with Cold Case Foundation. I am grateful for the opportunity that they are fulfilling my mission to find answers and justice on your behalf. I am just giving them credit for taking the time to respond to my emails and to at least try to help find answers. They are a nonprofit organization that helps the victims and/or victims' families of assault cold cases and only require that if you are applying to their website, you be family member and that you have obtained certain information for them to start researching the case. I know that there is a lot of controversy in the realm of using DNA or genealogy to help solve crimes since the Golden State killer was apprehended from using the databases to home in on the suspect. I will see where this path takes me and hopefully get some kind of answer that will ease the unknowing. I believe in the end, that is the worst part of this—not knowing. The fact that someone gets to walk around free while a family must suffer at another person's hands. Many know exactly what I am talking about, and some know that they will never have answers. I don't have words for that ending.

I am sending a follow-up email now with most of the information that they are asking for and will pray, cross my fingers, and do anything to help aid the universe in finding our answer. The likelihood is that the person is already dead or in prison for something else, but you never know, right? Like I stated earlier, I will continue to walk in gratitude, and something will come into focus; it usually does. I don't like that I am leaving things wide open with no closure. It is something that I don't have to give in this case. I always disliked stories being left open-ended, but it is what it is. Thank you for going along with me on this voyage.

Stephanie

PS—Here is a small token of some work that you created, and I wanted to share. I will always be extremely proud and blessed to be in your family.

Gallery of William C. Kolb's Work (some of it)

| Portraits of Bill Gaines | Portrait of Dr. Shearer-Richmond | Prominent businessman |

Head of Blood Bank of Virginia

| Unsure of name | Bill Kolb with portrait | Article with portrait |

More portraits that Bill Kolb created and took
pictures before giving them to the families.

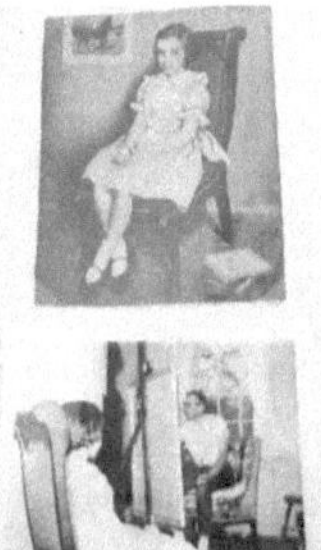

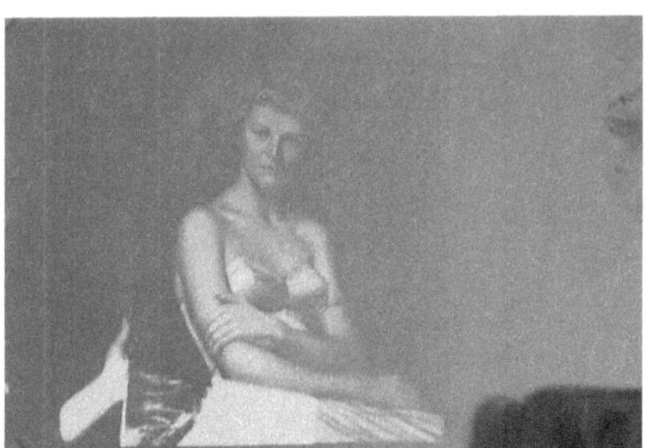

Portrait of Julia Simone (she took the
portrait back to England)

Bill Kolb in his studio

Article about
portrait

Son of Jay and
Kay, December
1972

John (brother
of Jay), painted
in Santa, Fe,
New Mexico
September 1973

This is the last creative work of art in March 1979. He painted Jean that is sitting in front the painting in the second picture. He painted the portrait from memory, as he remembered her as a young woman. There are others that I haven't seen in person or in pictures. I would love to see what else is out there.

WORKS CITED

Cold Case Foundation. 2023.

EPA United States Environmental Protection Agency. January 12, 2023.

Giodano, Amanda. "Why Trauma Can Lead to Addiction." *Psychology Today*, September 25, 2021.

GLAAD. 2023.

GLSEN. 2023.

Iti Fabvssa. 2017. "What is 'Iti Fabvssa'?" Choctaw Nation of Oklahoma.

Iti Fabvssa. 2018. "A Look Back: Oklahoma Presbyterian College." Choctaw Nation of Oklahoma.

"LGBTQ & Gay-Friendly Rehab Centers Near Me." 2023. americanaddictioncenters.org.

LGBT Life Center. 2023.

Native Land Digital. 2023.

National Black Justice Coalition. 2021.

Parker, Nakia. "Slavery, Labor and Resistance in the Choctaw Nation." *Presbyterian Historical Society, The National Archives of PC (USA)*, November 14, 2017. pcusa.org.

Priscilla Beach Theatre. 2023. 800 Rocky Hill Road, Plymouth, MA 02360, 508-224-4888. pbtheatre.org.

Rainbow Families. 2020–2022.

Remembering a Life. 2023.

Rezal, Adriana. "Where Most Native Americans Live." *US News and World Report.* November 26, 2021.

Stand in Pride. 2023.

The Trevor Project. 2023.

ABOUT THE AUTHOR

Stephanie Fisher is a first-time writer, seasoned ele-
mentary school teacher, and LGBTQ+ ally. She holds
a BA in developmental psychology and BA/MEd in
education and has always dreamed of being a writer.
Fisher is a native to the great state of Washington and
a proud alumni of Washington State University. Go,
Cougs!

9 798890 616074